WOMAN, WHO ARE YOU?

Woman, Who Are You?

Copyright © 2025 Cody Boyett

Scripture quotations from The Authorized (King James) Version. Rights in the Authorized Version in the United King-dom are vested in the Crown. Reproduced by permission of the Crown's patentee, Cambridge University Press.

This book is set in the typeface Athelas designed by Veronika Burian and Jose Scaglione.

Hardcover ISBN: 978-1-0881-2855-8
Paperback ISBN: 979-8-2967-0890-8

A Publication of *Tall Pine Books*
PO Box 42 Warsaw | Indiana 46581
www.tallpinebooks.com

| 1 25 25 20 16 02 |

Published in the United States of America

WOMAN WHO ARE *You?*

Cody Boyett

Table of Contents

Foreword

THERE ARE MOMENTS in life when the Spirit of God breathes on words, not just to educate us, but to awaken something that has been long buried beneath the noise of culture, pain, and misplaced identity. *Woman, Who Are You?* is such a moment. It's not simply a book. It's a divine summons—a trumpet blast to the daughters of God to come forth from the boxes they've been placed in and rise in the fullness of who He created them to be.

Written from a place of raw transparency and prophetic clarity, these words don't just speak—they pierce, they heal, they call you out and draw you in. With every page, you'll feel the heartbeat of a woman who has walked through shame, silence, and struggle, yet emerged with fire in her bones and truth in her mouth.

This book is not a set of rules to tame you. It is a mirror to see yourself rightly. It is a blueprint for restoration. And it is a love letter from a Father who never stopped knitting you together—thread by thread—with purpose, power, and peace.

Read this slowly. Let it stir you. Let it undo you. And let it remind you of the woman heaven always knew you were.

Introduction

I DIDN'T WRITE this book because I had all the answers. I wrote
it because I spent too many years tortured by the wrong ones.

I've wrestled with identity, felt the sting of rejection, and sat
under the crushing weight of expectations—some placed on me
by others and many I placed on myself. I've tried to fit the mold,
be the "right kind of woman," follow all the checklists, and still
felt like I missed the mark. And if you're anything like me, you've
probably asked the question too: "Who am I really?"

This book is my journey back to the beginning. Not just "my"
beginning—but "our" beginning. It's about returning to the place
where the Creator whispered your name before anyone ever
spoke it. It's about seeing yourself through His eyes instead of
your past. It's about uncovering the truth buried beneath pain, religion, and performance.

We'll talk about the woman in Genesis. The helper. The warrior. The image bearer. We'll dive into the Titus 2 and Proverbs 31 women—but not through the lens of comparison or condemnation. We'll look at them as God intended: pictures of His design, not burdens to carry. We'll examine what it means to contend, to nurture, to reflect, and to "become"—not in someone else's shadow, but in God's original intent.

This is not a manual for perfection. It's an invitation to wholeness.

So to the woman reading this—whether you're broken or bold, weary or wildly unsure—I pray you find yourself in these pages. Not the version of you shaped by shame or silence. But the version heaven dreamed up before the foundations of the world.

Let's begin the journey back to who you really are.

With love and expectancy,
Pastor Cody Boyett

CHAPTER ONE

A New Beginning

WHO ARE WE as women? Sometimes I think we try to get pigeonholed into one section, to fit one agenda or one narrative. God has a whole picture, not just a part. Sometimes we try to fit into a person's idea of what a woman is, and we feel really bad about ourselves, because we feel as if we can't ever live up to this person they're asking us to be. God tells us that we are created as a whole person and their idea is just one portion of our identity. People are really good at that. They're good at taking things they want and the things that they like and making a whole theology out of it. However, we want to look at the whole counsel of the Word of God. What does He say about us? How are we supposed to act? What are we supposed to do?

Oftentimes, we take the good things about us and try to get rid of them or we feel shame because they don't fit someone else's agenda, or there are things about us that are not so good, and we think they're okay. So this book will really be about ourselves. Who we are. Who God has created us to be. What are the positives? What are the negatives? Each of us have positives and negatives in our lives. Everybody has stuff that's really good, and others have traits that aren't so good. The not-so-good stuff either needs to be crucified or we need to allow God to take that and turn it into good.

I heard my husband say something that was very profound to me. He said that God deals with our sins right off the bat, the addictions and different things, but whenever He cleans us up and starts sanctifying us, then we have other things that He puts His finger on. I like to call those the nitpicky things. Someone once said to us, "Well, I get really angry, and I don't know how to fix it." My husband said, "That's because anger isn't just a fleshy thing, it's a spiritual thing, and you're trying to control a spiritual thing in a fleshy way." Anger is not wrong in and of itself. Jesus got angry in the temple and He overturned the tables when they were trying to prevent people from being able to pray. So anger is not the problem. The issue then comes when your anger isn't submitted to the Lord, and you operate in sin instead of operating by the spirit. That's when it becomes wrong.

God didn't call you to be a doormat. He called you to be a soldier. Soldiers can't fight if they can't get angry enough. We have a lot of things in our life that we deem are bad, but really they could just be spiritual things that we haven't submitted to the Lord yet, and we're trying to deal with those spiritual battles in fleshy ways.

We're going to talk about the law of first mention of women in the Scriptures. The law of first mention is the first time something was mentioned in the Bible. Wherever something is mentioned first in Scripture is how that theme or thing should be understood throughout the rest of Scripture. The law of first mention in Scripture of the woman is going to be in Genesis 2. The main thing I want to focus on is the beginning. The Lord told me, "If the beginning isn't fixed and if it isn't correctly understood, then everything that flows from it will be skewed." He said, "Go back to the beginning, to the root of it all. If you're going to understand who you are, you have to dig down to where you began."

In Genesis 1:1–2 (KJV), we see creation is beginning:

In the beginning God created the heaven and the earth. And the earth was without form, and void; and darkness was upon the face of the deep. And the Spirit of God moved upon the face of the waters.

I thought this was so profound because before God does anything, He always prepares the way. Before He does anything in your life, my life, or creation, before He ever even spoke a word, He sent His Spirit. He sent Holy Spirit to prepare the way. It may not always look like what it did at creation, but the way in which you go will always be prepared. He said, "I'll go before you and I'll make the crooked places straight." He goes before and makes a way. So His Spirit came before His word was ever spoken. His Spirit came out and it moved upon the waters. And whenever the atmosphere was ready, when the Spirit had prepared it to receive the word of God, then the word of the Lord came forth, and it accomplished what He sent it to do. And in every verse in every day of creation, God said, "Let there be, and there was." He spoke, "Let there be light, and there was light," "let there be a firmament in the midst of the waters, and there was," "let there be waters under the heaven be gathered together in one place, and let the dry land appear, and it was so," "let the earth bring forth grass, the herb yielding seed, and the fruit tree yielding fruit after its kind whose seed is in itself upon the earth, and it was so." And God said, "Let there be lights and the firmament of the heaven to divide the day from the night, let them be for signs and for seasons and for days and for years, and it was so." God said, "Let the waters bring forth abundantly the moving creature that has life and fowl that may fly above the earth and the open firmament of the heaven and it was so." And God said, "Let the earth bring forth the living creature after its kind, cattle and creeping thing and beast of the earth after its kind, and it was so." Everything that was created was created by the word of God. But then, we see that man is created. When man is created, he is not created by the spoken word of God. God speaks and says in Genesis 1:26 (KJV), "Let us make man in our image." Note that the Trinity is in the beginning: there is God the Father, God the Son, and God the Holy Spirit. God is conferring with the Spirit and the Son and He's saying, "Let us make man." "Let *us* put our hands on him."

We are the only things in this life that God has ever put His hands on to create. That's how important you are, that the hand of God has been upon your life from the moment you were first brought into this world. Scripture says, "Let us make man in our own image, after our likeness, so that they may have dominion over all the created things." So in this we see that God has an intended purpose. Not only did He create us by the works and movement of His hand, but He created us with a purpose in mind. You're not here for no reason. Genesis 2:7 talks about how He created man. It says, "Then the LORD God formed the man of dust from the ground." He formed him, which denotes a potter, like the potter that forms the clay. It continues, "And [He] breathed into his nostrils the breath of life; and the man became a living person." So not only did he put His word and His thoughts into mankind, He put His hands on us and then He put His mouth and His breath in us.

So He breathed and man became a living soul. We then see in Genesis 2:18 (KJV), where it says:

The LORD God said, It is not good that the man should be alone; I will make him a help meet for him.

This is where we get the term *ezer* from.
Genesis 2:21–25 (KJV) says:

And the LORD God caused a deep sleep to fall upon Adam, and he slept; and took one of his ribs, and closed up the flesh instead thereof; And the rib, which the LORD God had taken from man, made he a woman, and brought her unto the man. And Adam said, This is now bone of my bones, and flesh of my flesh: she shall be called Woman, because she was taken out of Man. Therefore shall a man leave his father and his mother, and shall cleave unto his wife: and they shall be one flesh. And they were both naked, the man and his wife, and were not ashamed.

So we see here the creation of woman. Woman was taken out of the side of man. She was taken from the side, not to be underneath the feet of man. She was not taken from the head of man to be over man. She was taken from the side of man so that she could be a partner, so that she could walk alongside him and fulfill what God had intended from the beginning. He created male and He created female. He knew exactly what He was doing.

When God made you who you are, He knew what He was doing. He did not make a mistake. He did not put you in the wrong body. He said you were a girl because you are a girl. Adam was a man because He knew that He wanted a man and He wanted a woman. He has created who you are on purpose, for a purpose. He wasn't confused. He is very intentional about what He's doing. Things tend to get confusing due to the consequences of letting sin have dominion after the fall of man. Perversion comes in and tries to twist and redefine what God had created in the beginning.

Remember, wherever we see something first mentioned in Scripture is the way it is meant to be understood. Man and woman.

Two genders. There were no multiplicities, no dualities, no alternatives. Everything was perfect the way He created it. The perversion of our sin nature gave birth to so many identities, personalities, pronouns, etc. Make no mistake, none of that was a part of His design. None of that was part of His plan for you. Nothing you have believed about life as you know it until now has any bearing on the freedom God wants to release to you now. This is not a psalm of hate or a slur to who you truly are. On the contrary, it is the sound of liberty to every false delusion and idea of this world that has caused you to believe you are or can be anything other than who God has said you are. This word right now is a key to unlock every chain and fetter that you've carried for so long that you can't even feel its weight anymore because you're so used to it. But not anymore, friend. Not after this day.

Go with me to Psalm 139:13–18 (KJV):

For thou hast possessed my reins: thou hast covered me in my mother's womb. I will praise thee; for I am fearfully and wonderfully made: marvellous are thy works; and that my soul knoweth right well. My substance was not hid from thee, when I was made in secret, and curiously wrought in the lowest parts of the earth. Thine eyes did see my substance, yet being unperfect; and in thy book all my members were written, which in continuance were fashioned, when as yet there was none of them. How precious also are thy thoughts unto me, O God! how great is the sum of them! If I should count them, they are more in number than the sand: when I awake, I am still with thee.

The psalmist is talking here, and he says, "Before I ever was, You knew me." Then Jeremiah 1:5 (KJV) says:

Before I formed thee in the belly I knew thee; and before thou camest forth out of the womb I sanctified thee, and I ordained thee a prophet unto the nations.

I want to focus on the part stating "before he formed me." We see that the God who was forming with His hands in the beginning is the same God who is forming now in Jeremiah's day. He was speaking to Jeremiah, but if He's doing it in Jeremiah's life, He's doing it in all of our lives. He has knit us together in our mother's womb. It's intentional. If I put my hands on something, it's because my brain says, "Let's do this." It's not something that just happened that created a human being. He didn't just "happen" upon Adam and Eve. He had purpose and intentions.

"Before I formed thee in the belly I knew you." That means before you were ever in your mother's womb, that in the heavenlies, you were there with Him. Does that mean I was there in my body? What does that mean? I can't honestly tell you that, but what I do know is that before you were formed in your mother's womb, you were living in the heart of God and that nobody is put on this planet by accident. And for you to correctly see who you are in God, you have to realize that you have been made by a Creator who loves you and has a purpose for you.

Your parents may have been surprised that you showed up, and people may have told you that you were a mistake. But people say wrong things all the time, so I just want to clear this up for you. People have sexual intercourse all the time, but unless God says, "You're going to have a baby," you're not having a baby. People want babies all the time, and they do everything right and they have all the things and do all the things in the right order, and they never conceive and have a child. Sometimes God says, "Not right now" or maybe "never." Then there are times people just do the things in sin and have babies. It doesn't seem fair or right. They don't want babies but they have them, and people who want babies can't have them. But God has a purpose and intention for everyone. So whether your parents wanted you and had you, or whether you were told you were a mistake and weren't wanted, you're not the only one that's ever felt like "nobody wanted me here."

When I was growing up, I got to a point in my life where I realized the circumstances surrounding my birth. My parents got married and my mom was very young. Not a child bride by any means, but just freshly out of high school when they decided to tie the knot. She didn't want to get married. Her home life was super strict. My grandparents loved the Lord, but sometimes they were very rigid in their beliefs and it became stifling to her to a certain extent. It was something I couldn't see until I grew up. I didn't understand what she had gone through because I had never experienced it myself. The day she got married, she said her hair was wet, and she cried and cried. She said she loved my dad but she just didn't want to get married, and that her parents made her go ahead and get married. There came a day in my life when I was a teenager and I was living with my dad and stepmom, and my mom called me on the phone and said, "When I found out I was pregnant, I was devastated." I was shaken to my core. I had never felt like a mistake, but I took that as she didn't want me.

She didn't want to be married, and she didn't want to have a kid. For a long time, the enemy really messed with me about that, because to feel that you weren't wanted was hard. It's what she had said, but it's not what she meant. She said when I was born, she loved me more than anything, but all I could ever hear from that point on was, she didn't want me. She loved me but didn't want me. And that does something to a person.

It's not just all these orphan kids. I had parents growing up, but just because you have parents doesn't mean that you can just feel that you are wanted. But whether they wanted you or planned for you to be here, whether a surprise or mistake, you were never that way in heaven. God fully intended on you being born right in the season that you were born. He intended on you living in the season that you're living, and He has a purpose in mind for your life—and it's not just breathing and waking up and going to sleep or work. God's purpose for you is bigger than that.

I'm not trying to portray my mom in any negative light. I love her, and I'm trying to understand her. If it's ever going to get made right, you have to try to understand, and that's "the thing" in my life. I just wanted to be heard. I never wanted to be hurt or understand where she was coming from, or what she had to say because I was hurt. And because the enemy planted that thought in my mind that I wasn't wanted, it threw everything into a tailspin. And because of that, I've always been a people pleaser and never wanted to make anyone mad or upset. It sent me into overdrive because now I had to prove that I was worthy to be here. I had to prove that I was good enough to be loved. I had to prove that I was good enough to be on this earth.

I thought about that later on in my life. I thought, *Wow, your wedding day is supposed to be the happiest day of your life, and she didn't even dry her hair.* For a long time, I had held some stuff against my mom because I didn't understand. And now that I'm older, I understand where she was coming from. Instead of trying to hate her or be mad at her for it, I started trying to see where she was coming from and started seeing what was going on in her life. And maybe I would've felt the same way if it were me in her shoes. She said she just wasn't ready and didn't know what to do with me.

None of those feelings that I went through was a part of her intentions when telling me that, but it was what the enemy used to trap me in this hamster wheel cycle. In just the last little bit, I've been able to break free from all that unforgiveness and resentment that I had toward her and be able to see her for the beautiful creation that God made her. And God is going to use all of our pain and our story and help heal us and His people. Neither one of us are perfect, but we're trying, and that's all that matters now.

He said He knit me together in my mother's womb, which means that I was woven together. Knitting is a handcraft. You can't just knit because you wish you could knit; you have to put your hands on it. I'm not a knitter, but I do crochet, and I want to tell you that when you crochet something, you know every stitch. You were there for every piece of it. You know where you missed a stitch in the blanket. You know where there's a gap, where it's tighter in some places or looser in some places. It may be because your rhythm was a little off. But God's rhythm was not off when He made you.

What I want to tell you is that He knows every single thing about you. He knows where there are things that are missing. He knows where there are things that seem like they don't fit just right. If you have those parts in your life, it's not because God made you a mess. It's because God left a hole there because there is something He intends to fill that hole with. When things aren't flowing just right, when your body's out of order, He knows how to fix it because He's the One that made it. When your heart is broken and you don't know how it's ever going to be put back together, the God that made you knows how to fix it.

We can go to people and look for affirmation and love and fulfillment, but we're never going to receive that, except from the

One who created us in the first place. You were never in my heart at the beginning because some of you were here before my beginning, but you were in *His* heart. You're in my heart now, and I love you now, but He's loved you always and created you with great purpose.

In Ephesians 2:10, it says,

For we are His workmanship, created in Christ Jesus for good works, which God prepared beforehand so that we would walk in them.

We're HIS workmanship. We are the work of HIS hands. Isaiah 64:8 says,

But now, LORD, You are our Father; We are the clay, and You our potter, And all of us are the work of Your hand.

I've met so many people in my lifetime. Maybe you're one of these people that you know God loves everybody. You know that God has a plan for everything and everyone. Yet, you can't imagine that He would love you, that He would care about you, and that He would give good things to you. You can be the workmanship of God's hand and not know if He really wanted to put His hand on you. You think to yourself, *Nobody else really has anything good for me, so how could I ever think that God has something good for me?* Thoughts like that are exactly what God desires to fix and set right in your perspective and in your thinking.

You need to fully understand that not just everybody else was created by God on purpose for good works; you were, too. You are the workmanship of His hands. You were created by God on purpose, for purpose. You have been knit together in your mother's womb.

I was looking up DNA images to see what it looked like, and it's basically two strands and they're all connected and woven together. At your conception, something happened in your mother's womb. An egg was fertilized and God began to knit. He began to take pieces of your mom and your dad, your grandpa and your grandma (for some of us, He reached way back and we have some traits from people we have never even met), and God said, "I'm going to take a little piece of this and that, and it looks like it's going to be good." And He made us. He knit us together and an egg began to look like a little peanut. And He just kept knitting, and a peanut started looking like a little alien. And He kept knitting, and kept nurturing, and kept feeding, and you kept growing, and He kept knitting until He said, "It's just right." Then after some time, you were delivered. You were here. But the hand of God has not stopped being on your life. He's still knitting and forming.

I love how Scripture says that we are the clay and He is the potter. He could've chosen any example of material that He wanted to choose, but He said, "I choose to talk about Myself as the potter and you as clay." It's one of the most easily formable materials. Even if the clay gets messed up, you can just squash it and start all over again. He just keeps putting His hands on it and keeps molding it, and He makes something beautiful and puts it in the fire, brings it out, and puts it back in the fire, and brings it out. And when it's finished, it's a vessel of honor that He can use for His glory and for His purpose.

Then we get to Isaiah 45:9–13, where it says,

"Woe to the one who quarrels with his Maker—a piece of pottery among the other earthenware pottery pieces! Will the clay say to the potter, 'What are you doing?' Or the thing you are making say, "He has no hands'? Woe to him who says to a father, 'What are you fathering?' Or to a woman, 'To what are you giving birth?'"

This is what the LORD says, the Holy One of Israel and his Maker: "Ask Me about the things to come concerning My sons, And you shall commit to Me the work of My hands. It is I who made the earth, and created mankind upon it. I stretched out the heavens with My hands, And I ordained all their lights. I have stirred him in righteousness, And I will make all his ways smooth. He will build My city and let My exiles go free, Without any payment of reward," says the LORD of hosts.

The Lord was saying that sometimes we get to places in our life that we argue with Him and we say, "Why did You even make me? Why did You even put me on this planet? I hate it here. Why did You let my mom and dad be my mom and dad? Why am I born in the family I'm born in?" And He says, "Stop striving with

Me." He has told us that He has a purpose. He's going to raise us up, build cities, set captives free. Why? Because He didn't just make us for no reason; He made us for a purpose.

Romans 9:20–21, which is New Testament as Isaiah was Old Testament, says,

> *On the contrary, who are you, you foolish person, who answers back to God? The thing molded will not say to the molder, "Why did you make me like this," will it? Or does the potter not have a right over the clay, to make from the same lump one object for honorable use, and another for common use?*

Verse 23 says,

> *And He did so to make known the riches of His glory upon objects of mercy, which He prepared beforehand for glory.*

We're in the book of Romans, but we're hearing the same thing we heard in Isaiah. Scripture says there's nothing new under the sun. They were complaining in the Old Testament, "Why did you make me?" and Paul said, "You're still striving with the same thing." All the years between the Old Testament and the New Testament, and even right now, we're still having the same argument with God. Even thousands of years now down the road, we're having the same thoughts in our head. "I don't want to be here," "I don't want to do this," "Why am I here?" But God said if we're ever going to fix that and get out of that mode of thinking, we have to go back to the beginning. Go back to the day you were created in your mother's womb and knit together. You have to look at it the way God looked at all of His creation, and after He created everything, He said, "It was good." And when He looked over at the man after He made him, He said, "That is VERY good."

Some of you look at the day you were born and you say it was not a good day. But God said you will never properly see where you're going if you can't look at that day and know that no matter what people were doing—no matter if they were on drugs, no matter if rape was involved, no matter if you were wanted or not, surprise or not, mistake or not—you have to look at that day and you have to say, "You know what? That's the day that I showed up. That's the day the purpose and the heart of God was brought to the earth. I was knit together in my mother's womb and THAT IS VERY GOOD!" People may not have had good plans or intentions, but God had the best plan in mind.

Jeremiah 29:11 says,

"For I know the plans that I have for you," declares the LORD, "plans for prosperity and not for disaster, to give you a future and a hope."

I also want to take you to Matthew 10:29, which says,

"Are two sparrows not sold for an assarion? And yet not one of them will fall to the ground apart from your Father."

Can you not buy sparrows for pennies? Yet not one of them falls to the ground without your Father. A bird who was worth pennies can't fall to the ground without God's hand being right there with it. He said, "But the very hairs of your head are all numbered." He's not just with you, He knows you. He's very well aware of you, very well acquainted with you. Before you were, He was. He knows you better than you know yourself. How many of you know the number of hairs on your head? I know I don't.

The Bible goes on to say, "So do not fear; you are more valuable than a great number of sparrows." You're worth more than what you believe. Sparrows don't set at liberty the captive, they don't build the kingdom of God, they're not the hands and feet of Jesus and the earth, but you are. You are the evidence that He is. Do some self-reflection. Look back on your beginning, the day you were created and born, and tell yourself that you're not going to look at this the way you have been looking at it your whole life. That you're going to allow God to show you that He created you and He made you. Let the Lord change your perspective; get alone with Him and let Him tell you Himself. He loves you. He made you with His own two hands. He made you exactly how He wanted to for the purpose that He has for you. You were made just right, with all of the potential for growth, for God's plan for your life to be fulfilled.

CHAPTER TWO

The Titus 2 Woman

I N THE LAST chapter, we talked about how if we are going to completely and fully understand who we are, we have to heal from the beginning. That no matter what circumstance we were born in, or who our parents were or weren't, what our upbringing was like, etc.—the fact is, God formed us and knit us together in our mother's womb. He said, "I want you to be here," and He had a purpose and said it was good. Everything that God created, He said it was good. And when He created man and woman, He said they were very good. So you need to know you were not a mistake. You were not unwanted. You were not abandoned. God had a divine design sending you to the earth at the time He did and to the people that He did, and everything that's happened in your life has happened so the purpose of God can be fulfilled in your life. Whatever you've been through, He intends to heal you of it. He intends to use it for a testimony to help someone else, and it's very good. The reality that you are here on this planet right now is very good, and it is God-ordained and God-orchestrated. No matter how you showed up, it's good.

Now that our view of beginning has been settled, we're going to be looking into the Titus 2 woman. Titus 2 and Proverbs 31 are usually the chapters used most by the enemy to make women feel guilty about all the things that we're not. I believe God has highlighted those chapters first, before we can go on, so that He can debunk the myths and hopefully correct some one-sided teaching that has been going on for some years.

Titus 2:1–5 says,

> *But as for you, proclaim the things which are fitting for sound doctrine. Older men are to be temperate, dignified, self-controlled, sound in faith, in love, in perseverance. Older women likewise are to be reverent in their behavior, not malicious gossips nor enslaved to much wine, teaching what is good, so that they may encourage the young women to love their husbands, to love their children, to be sensible, pure, workers at home, kind, being subject to their own husbands, so that the word of God will not be dishonored.*

I want to go over the first verse that says, "But as for you, proclaim the things which are fitting for sound doctrine." Doctrine is instruction. Paul is writing here to Titus, and I want you to understand the whole purpose of the book, because sometimes people use the Scripture to promote their own agendas, and I hate to say that, but it needs to be said. That way you can rightly divide what's going on in your life. Is it God saying it? Or is it people twisting what God said to fit their motives and what they want you to be? Are we seeking Him for truth or just regurgitating what we've heard all of our lives? For so long, people have twisted His Word to make it what they want. They have taken it out of context to promote their own agenda. I am not a feminist, nor do I think that women rule the world, but I do believe that we have a God-ordained place. I do not believe that we are doormats, or that we are to be under the foot of anyone, ever. I don't believe that the Scripture supports that in any way either. Sometimes it's preached to us that way, so if you've heard that, pray for the people, that God would open their eyes and that they would see the whole of it all.

That's what Paul is saying. He's writing this book for Titus, who is of Greek descent. He's not Jewish (or Hebrew), he is not from Rome, and he has a completely different kind of cultural background than Paul. Paul said he is writing to Titus in the faith. Titus has gotten saved under Paul's ministry, and Paul is going to put him in charge of the church at Crete. So Paul is putting him in charge of these churches, and the purpose of the book of Titus is to bring order to all of the home churches that were in Crete. You have to understand that Paul is not writing this because he wants to tell people what to do and how to be just because he wants to. The church in Crete is in chaos. So Paul is saying that number one, he wants Titus to set up leadership in the church, and number two, he wants him to bring correction to men and women.

God isn't correcting just one gender and not the other. If there are rules and guidelines for women, there are rules and guidelines for men. God is speaking to an issue, not just talking to women having issues, but everyone having issues, because God is not one-sided in anything that He does. He is well rounded, whole, together, and fitly joined because that's who He is and what He does. For God to be saying He needs Paul to bring order, He had to realize there was chaos, and there were things that were going on that didn't need to be happening.

In Titus 1, Paul is acknowledging Titus and how much he loves him, and how he's a son of the faith. And this is where we get those spiritual mothers and fathers. Paul was a spiritual father because, for those that got saved under him, he would raise them up and be that spiritual guide in their life. That's why you hear people today talking about their spiritual mom or dad. It's nothing creepy or weird, it's just who is teaching them how to do it. They follow them, as they follow Christ. Paul is writing this, first telling Titus he loves him and he is born in the faith, and then Paul speaks directly about qualifications for leaders. This is how a leader is supposed to be. Why is he telling him that? It's because there are leaders in power at the moment that are corrupt, so he's saying, "What you're seeing is not what's supposed to be, so I need to write down the things you need to be looking for in a person that says that they've got what it takes to be a leader."

Then he starts talking about the men and the women. He said, "Start teaching sound doctrine." Why? Because there's been so much corruption in the teaching and in the preaching, you're going to have to redirect everything.

I feel like that's what God is doing. There's been so much corruption, and in the area that I live in, it is very hard for women in ministry. People say, "You're not supposed to do that. You're not supposed to have authority over a man." And all those things are partially correct. Women are not supposed to usurp authority over a man. That doesn't mean that they can't be in leadership over a man. It just means they can't take it by force. When you take leadership by force, it's not correct. But if God places you in a position and a man comes in and says, "I can sit under you. I can glean from you. I can hear God through what you're saying, and I don't mind sitting under you," then that's okay. I believe that God is saying He wants us to speak the things that are suitable and proper for healthy doctrine. And that it's time to have a healthy view of ourselves as daughters of the King because it's been so twisted for so long.

I'm having to talk about all the things I really don't want to talk about, subjects that have kind of become taboo because of the way people have twisted them. God doesn't mean for those things to become taboo, twisted, or one-sided. He means for them to be healthy. I begin to think how often we have an unhealthy view of ourselves as women, and we feel all of this pressure telling ourselves things like, "You're a woman of God, so you're supposed to do this and that," and there's all these boxes you have to check off. And you think to yourself how you will never be that.

If you feel that way, that feeling is not coming from God. It's coming from people. His peace and His loving kindness does have correction, and there are times where God will tell us we need to straighten up. His correction, however, does not induce a sense of hopelessness but rather a desire to do better and become more than we are in our current state.

This is what God was using Paul to help Titus do. He said there were things that needed correction and they needed to talk about what was healthy and what was not. If it's going to be in God, it's going to be whole, and it's going to be complete. It's not going to be missing pieces and parts, and it's not going to be one-sided. You're going to have a total view. If we're going to understand the Titus 2 woman the way God wants us to, we have to know why it was even written.

Have you ever been in church and heard preaching and have been doing everything you could do the right way, and you hear someone talking about something that you don't have a problem with in yourself, yet you immediately start looking at yourself and thinking how you could do better? If you don't have a problem with submission, don't beat yourself up because you think you are not submissive enough. If you're living a holy life, don't beat yourself up and think you're not living holy enough. If you're not gossiping about people, don't tell yourself that if you saw so-and-so somewhere and told somebody about it that it would be gossiping; don't overthink it. There's always some-thing that we can take to the extreme, and that's what the ene-my is counting on. He's banking on the fact that we are going to take all the things that God meant in love, that were to be gen-tle corrections of things that were out of line or out of order, and that we take them to the extreme. That we mess ourselves up be-cause we get a goal in our head that we're never going to achieve, and then we will quit and give up. So, the Lord desires for us to understand the whole of Titus.

God brought me to Luke chapter 8 because I wanted to talk about everything that God does. He intends for it to be whole, healthy, sound, suitable, proper—not toxic.

Luke 8:40–47 says,

And as Jesus was returning, the people welcomed Him, for they had all been waiting for Him. And a man named Jairus came, and he was an official of the synagogue; and he fell at Jesus' feet, and began urging Him to come to his house; for he had an only daughter, about twelve years old, and she was dying. But as He went, the crowds were pressing against Him.

And a woman who had suffered a chronic flow of blood for twelve years, and could not be healed of anyone, came up be-hind Him and touched the fringe of His cloak, and immediate-ly her bleeding stopped. And Jesus said, "Who is the one who touched me?" And while they were all denying it, Peter said,

"Master, the people are crowding and pressing in on You." But Jesus said, "Someone did touch Me, for I was aware that power had left Me." Now when the woman saw that she had not escaped notice, she came trembling and fell down before Him, and admitted in the presence of all the people the reason why she had touched Him, and how she had been immediately healed.

This is amazing! This woman is coming, and she's having issues for 12 years of constant bleeding. No one's been able to help her. She has spent all of her money on physicians and yet no one's been able to help. She hears that Jesus is passing by the same way that Jairus has heard that Jesus is passing by. Jairus came first and said, "Will you please go to my house?" And Jesus said, "Absolutely." While on the way to his house, this woman said, "I've done everything that I know to do and nothing has helped," and in her desperation and hanging on to the last bit of hope that there was, she presses through the crowd and touches the hem of His garment, and immediately her blood stopped.

You can look at this a lot of different ways, but one of the things I want to bring out is that if you're here in the story, imagine that this is something that's happening to you today. If one person asks you for something, and then someone else comes in, we would say that it's rude, that they need to wait their turn. Jairus asked first. After all, that's what we teach our kids. That if someone's got something first, you let your child play with it only when the other one finished. We have this weird philosophy in our head because of the way we were taught to share, and yes, sharing is good, but Jesus is big enough to help everybody. We don't have to share the Lord. He is ours and we are His. He's big enough to take care of all of us at the same time. If every woman reading this began to pray right now, He could hear every single one of you in grave detail and not miss one word, and He would be able to touch us all at the same time.

So this woman has to deal with the crowd of people who are telling her, "There is a 12-year-old little girl that is sick, and here you are a grown woman, and you can't even wait your turn." We have all been through things where people tell us we're being ridiculous, when we're not. We may have legitimate needs and be hungry for something that is not being provided to us by anyone we're around, and we may be at the point of desperation and need help and are going to die, just like the bleeding woman. She just wanted to live, because if the blood would not stop flowing from her body, she would have died.

That's the thing! Here is the issue: Do you want to live? If you want to live and come to Jesus, don't let anything stop you. Don't let what people are going to say or think or feel stop you from coming to Jesus. It's not their life on the line, it's yours.

Not only is she being rude because she's touching Jesus out of turn, the fact that she's touching Jesus at all is an absolute no-no in their culture. If you were bleeding, you were unclean, you were not allowed to be touching the people, and the people were not allowed to be touching you. So if she touches Him, not only is she breaking the law, but she is making Him unclean by her un-cleanliness. We see here that she touches the border of His garment anyway. She presses through the crowd, and everybody that she presses through, she's got to touch on the way to get to Him. There will be times your mess is going to get on people, and it is what it is, because guess what? Sometimes your mess is going to get on me. Sometimes my mess is going to get on you. But if we can get through it and we can get to the source of our supplies, if we can get to Jesus, He can take care of the mess. All of the crowd wasn't in quarantine because she touched them, because when she touched Him she was healed. The fountain of her blood was dried up and there was no need for quarantine because she was clean. If she was clean, everybody else was clean. We're so afraid for people's stuff to get on us. But it doesn't matter if it gets on us, because as long as we can get them to Jesus, their issue can be healed.

What would have happened if the crowd would have just been understanding because she had a need? What if they just let her get by? Why don't we just help people on their way to Him?

You can look up the word *healed* and it says that it is being cured of a physical ailment, sometimes a spiritual thing. The healing covers both, but it's only specific to one issue. Jesus knew someone touched Him because He felt the healing virtue leave His body. When she touched Him, her faith grabbed a hold of what was inside of Him and she got it. When the woman who didn't want to be seen or noticed saw there was no way to get out of this confrontation without telling the truth, she got up and said it was her. She confessed that she had been bleeding for 12 years and He was there and she had to try, and when she touched Him, all the blood dried up and it was finished. Twelve years of living in hell. Being alone. She was unable to hug anyone, touch anyone, connect with anything outside of the four walls in her home—except for the doctor. But now, it was over; she was healed.

Then Jesus said this to her in Luke 8:48: "Daughter, be of good comfort, your faith has made you whole. Go in peace." The healing came first, but Jesus doesn't leave anything undone. All throughout the Scripture, He asks people if they want to be made well. He asks that to men and women. I'm using the bleeding woman as an example because we're talking about "Woman, who are you?" We're women. We have issues, and Jesus can heal your issue. The greatest thing about it is, He doesn't just want you healed. He says, "Daughter, be of good comfort, be excited, be happy and at peace, because your faith has made you whole."

Whole means that you are saved. You are healed. You are preserved, and you are rescued. Jesus didn't want to just touch the issue in her body, He wanted to save her life. Not just physically, but He wanted to touch her inside and save her emotional and mental health. He wants to rescue us from all the places that we've been to let us know that we are saved, cured, and restored, and that everything we've lost is recovered. We are not just healed but have been made complete. You can be healed and still have emotional issues, still have the trauma that goes along with the illness or sickness or whatever the situation is. You still have the emotional issues and baggage that comes along with your situation.

But Jesus doesn't want to just take care of the main issue. He wants to take care of everything. That's the point I feel we are at. Where God is wanting to not just take care of our little issues, when we may need to do a little better here or a little better there; He wants to completely restore you from the very beginning. He wants you to see your beginning as good and wants to take everything that people have used to twist and pervert the gospel to make you into what they want you to be instead of what He says you are to be. He wants to make you whole. He wants to give you every single aspect of who you are one piece at a time, and when we get to the end of it, you can see it as a great big picture and not just the bits and pieces that people want you to see because it fits their agenda.

You can also see in Luke 8:49–56 that Jesus does make it to Jairus' house. His daughter is dead, but really it is for the glory of God. A 12-year-old girl and a woman with an issue of blood for 12 years. The number 12 in Scripture represents government. There was a government of sickness that had taken root and taken the throneship of these two daughters' lives. Jesus said on that day, the government was being shifted. That they weren't going to live in that issue and be ruled by it anymore. That He was going to save, heal, restore, preserve, rescue, and become the government that rests upon their life.

At 12 years old, this innocent beautiful girl was killed by something. She fell ill. There is something the enemy hates about purity and holiness and innocence and that was everything that the young girl represented. But Jesus came and healed her in her body. He resurrected her and brought her back to life. That is what God is doing with us. He is taking where we have been ruled by our issues and by what people have said that we need to be and what we don't need to be, and He is healing it and dethroning that mindset and giving us a new mindset and bringing us back to a place of purity, like the 12-year-old girl. He is bringing us back to that place of innocence and childlike faith, that we would hear Him and know His voice and be able to distinguish the truth from a lie, and that He would be able to reestablish all of it. It's a powerful thing.

Now that we see why the book of Titus was written, and that the purpose of the book is to give us a picture of the whole of who we are supposed to be, it's a lot easier to swallow when you realize the purpose behind what God is saying and that He's not just saying it to say it or to be mean. Some of us have a problem with rebellion because of how we were brought up. We were raised up under the thumb of someone else and now when we're grown up, we're just going to do our own thing. People aren't going to tell us what to do. When we hear passages of Scripture like this, we tend to put up a wall because we don't want to be tricked. We want to keep just doing us and being us.

Going back to Titus 2:3, it says, "Older women likewise are to be reverent in their behavior, not malicious gossips nor enslaved to much wine, teaching what is good." So, who are the older women? Does that just mean all the old ladies? No. That means mature believers and mature women in Christ. You might be 30, but you've been saved your entire life, and then a woman comes into the church who is 60 years old, but she's never been saved; you are the elder in that situation. You are the more mature woman in the faith. Can her life experience teach you some things? Absolutely. But as far as what pertains to godliness and sound doctrine and healthy teaching, you are the scholar in that situation. It's okay for younger women to help older women. It's not so much about the age as it is the maturity in the faith. Mature women in Christ are supposed to be reverent in their behavior. What does that mean? That means their behavior and conduct needs to reflect that of Christ. That we are not supposed to be portraying our own selves, and that everything we do, we want Christ to be seen in that—not malicious gossips, which means slanderous, false accusers, or in modern terms means you want to spill the tea.

If you're saying that you saw someone at the doctor, that's not gossip. That's not you talking bad about someone or saying anything negative about them. Malicious gossips are "I heard such-and-such" or "Have you heard yet?" Living in a very small town, or small office buildings, schools, etc., things make the circle. There is a ring and it gets around. Whether it's true or not, it gets around. As mature women and believers in Christ, we are not supposed to participate in that. Prayer request time at any women's meeting is not a place to start gossiping. Nor is it the place to disguise someone else's misfortunes as a prayer request so that you can let your small group in on the latest news. I have been to some meetings where people will ask for prayer for someone, and then go into detail about that person's life and what is "possibly" happening. That is slanderous and malicious gossip. If somebody needs prayer, you can pray for them. Sometimes we feel like we can pray better if we know the details. That's not always the case. Sometimes, you are just nosey.

I had someone message me once asking me to pray for a yes or no answer for her from the Lord. She said she couldn't go into detail, but that I was going to be the confirmation for her. I did not think that was going to happen, but the Lord spoke to me about it, because He knew in detail, and I told her what I felt like the Lord was saying. It wasn't a yes or no answer, but I heard specific things, and when I told her, she said it was the exact same thing God told her. She said she knew I was going to be that confirmation for her and she was right. So you can pray and not know the details, because God knows the details about everything. There is a time for detail, and a time to refrain. If it sounds like gossip, don't give the specifics. Just ask to pray for someone or say you have an unspoken request.

"Do not be enslaved to much wine." When you look up what the word *enslaved* means, it means don't be in bondage. Don't be drinking all the time. If drinking wine is leading to you drinking a bottle, you have a problem and need to ask God to help you. If you can't have a little wine, and it not turn into a lot of wine, it might be best to just not have the wine at all. As a pastor, I don't drink at all. Not because it's right or wrong, or because it's heaven or hell. I'm not more holy or righteous than anyone. But because of the position God has placed me in, if people see me do that, they might lose confidence in me. No matter how great of a person I try to be or how many good things I do, if people see me drinking, I'm done. I can't minister to them anymore. It's about how their perceptions are of me. I'm not trying to preach anyone to hell for having a little glass of wine, but don't say that God said a little wine is good for the stomach and then go on to drink a whole bottle everyday and think God is pleased with that because He's not. The Bible says "teaching what is good" and "that they may teach the young women to be sober." He is saying that the mature believers need to do all of these things so that you can speak into someone else's life. It's not about being so good because He needs you to be so good. It's about following these guidelines so you have the authority to speak into people's lives and they will receive you.

I was counseling with someone once and told them because of the way they love people that they have earned the right to speak into those people's lives. This was because she treated them the same all the time. She wasn't acting holier than anyone. She stood her ground on what God says and people respected her and saw her living things out to the best of her ability. People will hear that kind of walk. If you're not following the precepts of the Word and try to talk to people, they will tend to shut their ears off. Scripture should not be viewed as a bunch of rules that restrict us from being who we want to be, but rather as a written guide to help us become more Christlike and be able to bring more people to Christ. This is because we have been saved by the blood and cleaned up through the power of the Word and His Holy Spirit. We can't help other people if we have all of this mess in our life. Knowing we can be a benefit to someone else makes it easier to let go of certain things, because who doesn't want to help people? Who doesn't want to be able to speak into somebody's life and things change? We all want that. We were created to help.

That's why God says in Titus 2:4–5 that mature believers need to be this way, "so that they may encourage the young women to love their husbands, to love their children, to be sensible, pure, workers at home, kind, being subject to their own husbands, so that the word of God will not be not dishonored." It says to us, "Older women, teach what is good so that you may encourage the young women." It teaches that we're not lording over other people. Instead, we should be encouraging them and urging them on to do good works by the example of our life. Not just the words that are coming out of our mouths, but the actions that are following what we're saying. That we can cheer people on and say, "Girl, you can do this. I know you want to give your husband a piece of your mind today, but love your man. I know he is getting on your last nerves because I've been there. But you're going to make it over this hump. This is just a moment; this isn't your whole life."

Sometimes it feels like you've maybe had this issue for 12 years, but God. There will be a moment that He will come in and help that man. God will give you grace. Just keep loving Him, love your husband, love your children, be of sound mind, be sober.

Sobriety is not just sober as in, "Well, I don't drink anymore and I don't smoke anymore." Sober means that you are in your right mind. That your mind is not in chaos all the time. And when you are a young, new believer, there are so many voices fighting for your ear. As soon as you surrender your life to Christ, hell is on the warpath to get you back. Hell is coming to try to get you off course, God's trying to speak, and everybody is talking at the same time, and your mind is just going crazy. So you, mature believer, are the voice in the young believer's life that needs to say, "Hey, girl! Focus. Keep your eyes on Jesus. Don't worry about what everybody is saying. Just keep following Jesus one step at a time." If you're married, you must love your husband, even if he's not saved. God can save him. His journey to Jesus may not look like your journey to Jesus. Women usually just do things faster than men. There are some things that guys do faster, but the majority of things, including falling in love with Jesus, just come more naturally to women. That's because we are more emotional, and by nature, we want to have fellowship and build relationships.

Love your children. How? What is loving them? It's not just walking around telling them you love them. It's all of the things that you do that show love. Love is an action word. When you show up for them, when you cook for them, when you wash their clothes, whenever you go do things or go to church, when you teach them about Jesus or pray with them—that's how you love them.

To be sensible, and in your right mind, and have self control, and be pure and holy. We can't teach people to have self control if we don't have self control. So many people feel like if they are not a stay-at-home mom, they are failing their family. And some feel like if they are a stay-at-home mom, they are failing everything else. And that's just not the case. If the Lord has blessed you and you're able to be a stay-at-home mom, praise God. Sometimes it gets lonely and overwhelming, but God will send relationships in your life at the right time to pour into you when you need it and give you some human interaction that has nothing to do with crayons, snacks, lunches, *Bluey*, or YouTube. God will send you the things that you need, and until He does, He will be everything you need if you allow Him to be.

If you have to work outside the home, you can still work in your home. If you have a job outside of your home and you have a maid, you're still a good mom and wife. If you have to pay somebody to do the laundry and all the things, you're still a good mom and wife. The work is getting done, and it doesn't matter how it's getting done, as long as it's getting done and you're not leaving your family out to the wind. The work at home isn't just cleaning the toilets, scrubbing the showers, doing the laundry, and cooking. It's about building your children in the faith, building up your husband, and telling him all the good things and not just the negatives, because whatever you feed in his life, that's what's going to grow. Accentuate the things that he does well, give him those positive affirmations, and tell him you're proud of him. When he does something nice, even if it's rare, acknowledge that. Men love positive reinforcements.

Our homes are a ministry, as well. It's not just building up the earthly home and the things in it, it's about building up and working with the people that are inside of that home that God has given you. Building the relationships with your family and speaking life into the people that are around you all the time. I think sometimes women believe when they are not able to be a stay-at-home mom that they are total failures. On the other hand, stay-at-home moms think because they're not able to go out into the workforce that they're not helping their husbands. That's the enemy's goal. To get you to look at yourself and think you're the worst, but you aren't. Things are getting done the way they have to get done and that's okay.

I believe that building the people within the walls is much greater than scrubbing the floor. So, if you have to pay to get some help because you can't get it all done yourself, and God has blessed you with the funds to get someone to help you, do it. And if you don't have the funds to hire someone, phone a friend. Tell them that you understand it's not their responsibility, but if they could just help for a couple of days, I'm sure they would. Pray and ask God who you can invite into your home to be your sister and friend who won't judge you or look at you weird. Someone that if they help you, you can help them.

Kindness. It's a thing! Be kind to everyone. You don't know what they're going through. Kindness and love go a lot further than you think. I saw a sign once at a church that said, "Everything responds to love," and it's true. It's scientifically proven that everything responds to love. Plants respond to love. You can talk negative to a plant and it will shrivel up and die, or you can talk positive to a plant and it will just thrive and grow. If love works like that with your fern, imagine how it could work with people.

"Being subject to their own husbands," or "to be obedient to their own husbands" (as some versions of Scripture say)—what does that mean? That means that you are submitting to your own spouse, keeping in mind that this is written because things are out of order. If you're already submitting to your spouse, don't overthink it. If you're already being kind, then you're already being kind. If you're already living a pure and holy life, you're winning. And if you're not, He's just telling us to trim off what is not producing good fruit and continue to grow in the faith. None of this is for condemnation. This is for growth. If there are things in your life that don't need to be there, He is going to clip them off so that something better can grow in its place. We can't get new life out of a dead branch, so we cut off the dead branch, purge it, and grow good things.

This isn't a beat up session. It's a growing session so we can get new life sprouting. "Being subject to their own husbands, so that the word of God will not be dishonored." This means if I'm going to be subject to my own husband, I'm going to follow the rank. Our husbands are our covering. Even if you think there are holes in your covering, get your Holy Ghost patch out and begin to cover them up, because you're under the covering, and God is over the covering. You're under the covering of your own husband—not someone else's, but your own. You don't go by the rules of someone else's house, but the rules of your house.

So you're under the covering of your husband and you might be thinking, *What is up with this guy? What in the world?* But as God is teaching you who you are, pray for him, that God will begin to show him who he is, because God didn't say how women should be and leave out how a man should be. The man is brought up in Titus 2:2, and brought up again in Titus 2:6. We need to trust that while God is trying to show us who we are, God will also begin to show him who he is. Just take your prayer and let it be your Holy Ghost roof patch. Take the holes in him and fill them with prayer, and God will begin to deal with it from the perspective He sees, and He sees the whole thing. You only see the underneath. We don't have a clear perspective, even as much as we think we do. God can deal with all the things above the covering that we don't see: the brains, the emotions, the irrational, the stubborn, and all the things we may not like. He can deal with it and sometimes He will change them, and other times, He will change us. But either way, we're going to fall in line.

How do I say that this is okay? It's because I have submitted myself, even in toxic situations. Not just in my home, but in ministry. How is that godly? How would God have us submit to ungodly leaders? Because David submitted to Saul. David never took the kingship from Saul even though God ordained him king. He submitted himself unto Saul while Saul, demon-possessed, was throwing javelins at him. While he was going through all these things, Saul was still sitting on the throne. David loved Saul, and he prayed for Saul, and when it came down to when David was about to lose his life, God made a way for David to escape. So whenever there needs to be an escape, God will provide an escape. Until then, love them, pray for them, and trust God with them.

There came a time in my church life where I submitted until God delivered. He delivered me and brought me out, and I don't ever have to go back again. He put me in a spacious land, in a free place, and I still pray for them and love them, but I don't live there anymore. Even in my marriage. My husband and I have been doing marriage counseling, which is so weird because I never thought that would even be a thing, but God used every bad thing that we've ever been through and turned it for good. He's using it to help other people. There was a time in my life when I didn't agree with everything my husband was doing, and vice versa, but I loved him and I prayed for him anyway. Not all the time did I pray for him like I should have, because I was mad. Sometimes I yielded myself more to the flesh than I walked by the spirit. But I never gave up. Even on the days where I was letting my flesh live more than my spirit man, I didn't give up. And maybe if I let my spirit man live more than my flesh man, we could've gotten better quicker, but I digress. Are we perfect? No. But am I happy to be under the covering that I am? Yes. All the holes that I saw are not big gaping tears anymore. There are still some pin holes here and there, but that's okay because it's going to get better. Why? So that the word of God is not dishonored.

There are things that happen in marriage that call for your own safety to be a priority. You may need to get out of certain situations, and that's understandable. I'm not telling anyone to stay in an environment where you are being physically assaulted to the point that you are going to die or that you're in fear for your life. I'm not saying you have to stay if you're being cheated on with everybody. There are times that God permits you to walk away. I know women that have walked away and I know women who have stayed in all the situations. I've heard testimonies from both sides. So before you do anything, you pray and you ask God what He wants you to do and then follow Him. He will lead you to stay and give you the grace, or He will lead you out and give you the grace to go. It takes grace to do either one. It takes strength to do either one. We just don't want the word of God to be dishonored. We should want what God has given us, not just for ourselves, but for our homes, marriages, children—everything—we should want it to reflect Him because that's the point. We should want everything in our lives to reflect all of Him, and a lot less of ourselves.

Being a Titus 2 woman is going to call me into a place of growth, change, and submission. All that God is requiring of us is for Him to be able to change us from the inside out, so that others around us may also be changed. Titus 2 is not a cage we are trapped in or a thumb that we are pressed down underneath. Rather it is a place of surrender and submission to God, a holy submission to our husbands, and a place of freedom to speak into the lives of others once our lives are aligned with His word and will for us. Yes, Titus 2 is a place of freedom! Be released from the cages built by men and women by their misinterpretations of Scripture mingled with their biases and prejudices. Daughters of Zion, the thumb of harsh law has been lifted from off your heads and you are now mantled with truth. A crown of peace has been placed on your heads where the weight of judgments used to reside. You are not being dismissed from the mandate of His word when rightly divided. You are being sent out to do the will of Him who has called you. To bring honor to His word, to bring blessing to your families, and to bring life to those you encounter on your journey. May Titus 2 never again be used as a weapon against you. May it forever be a joyful journey that you walk on throughout your life to becoming more like Christ. A tool to sanctify you (to teach you in truth and love) and a mirror in which to behold yourself to see how far you have come and how far there is yet to go.

CHAPTER THREE

The Proverbs 31 Woman

I'VE HEARD ABOUT Proverbs 31 my whole life, and I've read it several times, I've heard it preached several times, and I've also heard people talk about it several times. It's all these things that a woman of God is supposed to be. She sells all the things, makes all the things, gets up early and cooks all the things and feeds all the people. She never sleeps or needs sleep because she's amazing. We may read these things and think, *I will never be that. That's not me. Where do I fit in that?* The first thing God said when we were going to start going over this to me was, "Stop looking at everything you're not, and start finding yourself in this passage. Start finding the things that you are good at." So I started reading it and was like, "Well, I still don't see me. I still don't understand me in this passage of Scripture or where I fit or belong." So I began to pray and ask God to stop letting me look at this from the lenses of what I've been taught and heard all my life, to let me see it for what He wants me to see it as. As I began to do that, God opened up so much, and I'm so excited about it.

Proverbs 31 was not written as a checklist for women. It wasn't meant to read it and tell yourself to check this box and check that. At the very first part of Proverbs 31, it talks about King Lemuel, who is telling about a prophecy that his mother had given him about how he should live his life, who he should marry, what he should and shouldn't do. It was like instructions on how he was supposed to live. After verse 9, it stops talking about Lemuel, and it goes into this explanation of a woman. This woman isn't an actual person. The Proverbs 31 woman is exactly like what Paul was giving to Titus, when he was telling them what to look for. In other words, the qualities of a good woman. If you want to know if someone is following Jesus, look and see if there's evidence in their life. They don't have to have it all, but if there's something in here about them that matches this description, then you know she's a good, godly woman.

We have taken this list of attributes and turned them into an idea of what women must be to be accepted and respected. For so many years, it has been an insurmountable task that has overwhelmed the daughters of God. After diving into this super heroine of a woman, I pray that we are filled with hope that we are not as far away from her as we have been led to believe. I pray that the chase for perfection and all striving will cease, and we can finally rest in the truths of this passage and thrive in the relationship we have with Jesus.

We're going to start in Proverbs 31:10, where it says,

An excellent wife, who can find her? For her worth is far above jewels.

I wrote this in my journal as I began my studies: "Who can find an able and efficient woman?" *Able* or *efficient* means having or showing high, moral standards. Basically, who can find a good woman? Who has beliefs and who stands up for those beliefs? Who isn't swayed by the things of this world but knows who she is and knows who she believes in? Who can find one of those? The Bible says there's nothing new under the sun. We think that our time today is worse than any other time, and the sin may look a little bit different, but the heart and the nature of people has always been the same. There have always been people who were liars, cheaters, and deceivers, from the very beginning until now. Back then, they were looking around asking who could find a woman who had morals, who was able, capable, and efficient in what she was doing. Who could find that? If she can be found, Scripture says, "Her worth is far above jewels." The King James Version of the Bible states, "Her price is far above rubies." This passage is probably the one that we're most familiar with.

For most of my life, I have envisioned this Scripture as beautiful red rubies. That virtuous woman with high moral standards is this precious gem. But when I began to dive down into it, "Her price is far above rubies" is not even what the word actually is. That was just the best they could come up with when they were translating it. The word is actually, "Her worth is far above pearls." When I found that out, I thought, *Okay, well, that's cool to know. It's not rubies or just random jewels, it's pearls.* As I was diving into that a little more, I found that rubies come from the earth. Most gems come from the earth. They're minerals that come from the ground. They are earthy. Pearls, though, are formed in the belly of an oyster. They come from something that has been buried in the dark. These particular pearls are not formed in shallow oysters, either. The pearls that are the most valuable are the pearls that are in the oysters that are found anywhere from 48 to 128 feet deep in the ocean. God said that a virtuous woman is not one that is earthy, she cannot be replicated by the standards of this world. A virtuous woman is more valuable than something that has been buried in the darkness, that God has been polishing and making in the deep depths of Himself, the depths of the water. What is even more profound is that water has always been representative of the Spirit of God. Buried in the deep, dark, remote location.

It has been said, "When you feel like you've been buried, you've really just been planted," and that God is doing something through the Holy Spirit on the inside of your life. Pearls that come from the ocean are more valuable than diamonds and rubies because they are rare. It's not hard to find a woman here that wears a Christian T-shirt or says she goes to church or Bible studies, but it is hard to find a woman who is capable, able, and efficient, with moral standards. High, godly standards of living—that has been buried in the secret place with her God and the power of the

Holy Ghost who has done a work in her life. Christian T-shirts are cheap. But a real life relationship with the Holy Ghost? There is nothing in this world that is comparable to it.

When searching out pearls, I thought about Matthew 13:45–46. It says:

> *Again, the kingdom of heaven is like a merchant seeking fine pearls, and upon finding one pearl of great value, he went and sold everything that he had and bought it.*

Keep these words in mind as we continue. All our lives we have been taught rubies, but no one dared to dive down deep to find the pearl. We see in the New Testament, Jesus is bringing up pearls again and saying when a merchant man finds a pearl of great price, when he finds the one that was in the deepest depths of the ocean—the one that's real, not the one that's created by man—he will know it.

Mikimoto, a company who sells, harvests, and manufactures pearls, and the founder of the company, Kokichi Mikimoto, would find a way to create them quicker. He would take pearls and pre-plant them in an oyster, then bury them in the ocean, not as deep as they would normally be. And he would leave them there for five years and would harvest them. It takes a skilled jeweler to be able to tell the difference between a deep water pearl and something that was recreated by man.

It's going to take the discernment of the Holy Spirit to really see who's got the goods and who is the real deal, versus who has been decorated by people and by themselves. We don't seek to be adorned to our own selves; we seek to be adorned by the Holy Spirit.

So as it said in Matthew, when he found that pearl of great price, he went and sold everything that he had, and he bought it. Why? Because the pearl of great price was of more value to him than everything that he owned. A woman who is really in tune with God and has surrendered herself and has given her life fully to Him is worth more than everything else. It's worth more than the house, the car, the clothes, the job, the people—everything.

Why does He say a pearl? The Lord revealed this to me several years ago. Most women want to be a diamond, until I found out that diamonds are a dime a dozen. Then they want to be like gemstones, so rubies really fit because gemstones are more expensive and precious than even the diamond. Why does God say the kingdom of God is like a pearl? Why does He say a woman who fears the Lord and is virtuous is of more value than all the pearls? It's because a pearl has to be taken in its entirety for it to have any value. You can have a big diamond and bust it up into a bunch of little diamonds, and it still has value. But if you break a pearl, it loses value completely. So you must take the whole truth of God. He said when he found that pearl of great value, he sold everything that he had because he needed the entirety of what it was, the wholeness of the kingdom of God. We can't take bits and pieces of the gospel that suit us and create something that will be valuable. We have to take Jesus and the whole truth and counsel of the Word of God for it to ever become effective and valuable in our lives and for it to bring forth fruit.

Proverbs 31:10–11 says,

An excellent wife, who can find her? For her worth is far above jewels. The heart of her husband trusts in her, And he will have no lack of gain.

This means she is of high integrity, that the heart of her husband safely trusts in her. Can we take it further? It means he doesn't worry about anything. He goes to work, provides, and brings home the money. He knows that when he gets home, she is such a good woman who trusts the Lord that she is going to be a good steward of what's brought into that house. Nowadays, both people usually have to work if you're going to make it, or you've got one person working and one that is an extremely good steward over the finances that are coming in the house because it almost takes two incomes to make it. I began to think about it and wondered, *Well, does it really take two streams of income, or are we just bad stewards of what God has given us?* We can probably do a lot better if we try. There's some things that we've got that we may not need, so we need to start thinking about that.

The King James Version told us, "The heart of her husband doth safely trust in her, so that he shall have no need of spoil." He doesn't have any need to go out and take anything from someone else to make ends meet or to make it work. Spoil is ill-gotten gain. Anything we take unlawfully from another person, or anything we take from the wreckage of someone else's calamity, and claim as ours is spoil. His heart trusts in her that what they have will be "gain" to him, and will not create a vacuum-like void in his life that he will constantly be trying to fill.

It's not just that we're being a good steward over the financial things; it means we're being a good steward of the emotional things of our homes. That we're being who we need to be for him so he doesn't have a need to go out looking for something else when he could be getting that from home. That means intimacy. It's supposed to be in your house. No, he doesn't need to be mean to you. Yes, he needs to love you. Yes, he needs to meet your emotional needs, as well. No, you're not just expected to lay down and be intimate when he's not doing anything that he is supposed to be doing. I'm not saying any of that. Intimacy is a two-way street, and both parties must give to make it work. I am saying that if he's doing his best to line up with God's Word, you need to be doing your best to line up. If you don't want him to be looking outside of the house, you don't need to be rebellious or withholding, because that's not scriptural. There is a balance, and there is a healthy medium, and you need to communicate with each other about all of these things. Healthy communication brings understanding and nurtures trust in our spouse. It's that he trusts in her that when he comes home, that it's going to be home. That he's fought hell, the world, and the people in it, and when he comes home, he doesn't need to be fighting you too.

There's a Scripture in the Bible, Proverbs 21:9, that says,

It is better to live on a corner of a roof Than in a house shared with a contentious woman.

"The heart of her husband does safely trust in her" means that when he comes home, it's not a warzone. There are times in our lives (those who have been married can say this) that every argument and fight wasn't all his fault. Yes, there have been times where it was his fault, but not all the times was it all his fault, and that we were bitter. Not even at him, but for all the things we have been through in our life because we haven't let God heal us yet. Maybe you are bitter right now because you're not allowing God to touch the things in your life that need to be healed. Your husband would rather live on the roof than live in the finest, most beautiful home with you because you need to let God do what He is trying to do in your life. When you let God heal you, you get a lot more peace within you.

And if you're not married yet, then you need to understand that you need to go into it having allowed God to already heal you. You need to take pointers from this, that if God has a plan of marriage over your life, ask Him to not let you be that girl, and let yourself hear what He is saying. Take wise counsel and instruction, and let your life be better before you get into it. There are still going to be things when you get married that will pop out to you, and you're going to have to deal with those things as you go, but for the most part, ask God to let you get as clean and healed as you possibly can before you go that way.

Proverbs 31:12 says,

She does him good and not evil All the days of her life.

She is a benefit, and not a misery and distress, to him all the days of her life. In your head you may be thinking how he is a misery and distress to you, so why can't you be a misery and distress to him? We're not talking about him today, we're talking about us. A person who can never own that they have faults, a person that can never admit that the problem isn't always somebody else, that always has to place blame onto another person, is not a full adult yet. Adults take ownership of what their issues are. You can never make him change. You can't make anyone change. But you can allow the Lord to change you. And whether they change or don't change, that's on them. But we have a responsibility and a duty to the Lord, that when He puts His finger on something in our life, we become obedient and don't live in open rebellion against what He is trying to do in us.

Proverbs 31:13 says,

She looks for wool and linen, And works with her hands in delight.

I read that and wondered what in the world we would need wool and linen for? Why is she seeking wool? This woman has servants. She seeks wool and linen and works willingly with her hands. What this means is that the people that are around her, she doesn't want them to have idle time. She wants to make sure they have everything they need, so she gathers all the materials they need so when they show up to work, they can do their jobs efficiently, so they're not hunting and scrambling for materials.

"She works with her hands" means that she's not expecting everybody else to do it by themselves. She will jump in the middle with them, get dirty, and be hands on with everything that's going on. You may not have servants, but there are people in your lives—maybe your kids or husband—and they need things to help their life go more smoothly. Maybe you're that person that steps in and knows that they need things, so before they ever even ask, you can have it out on the table for them. You know where their backpacks are, their lunch boxes are packed, their field trip money is on the counter, there's money in your account so you can tell your husband how much is available to spend. Let's look at it that way. What if you don't have employees or a husband or kids? Well, there may be people around you at your job, and you help look out for them. I had someone who worked for me, and when she first started working for me, she didn't really know a lot about it, but she watched everything that I did, and eventually, before I even needed anything, she was handing it to me because she knew by my actions what I was about to do next. So if you find those qualities in your life, those are good things. Helping people is good, godly, and right.

Proverbs 31:14 says,

She is like merchant ships; She brings her food from afar.

Everybody back in the day wanted to see the merchant ships coming. Why? Because they had all the good stuff. They had new clothes and food, and they brought stuff the people had never seen before. So they couldn't wait for the merchant ships to come. It says she is like the merchant's ships—not one ship, but the fleet of them. When you see her coming, you know that she's got something for you that you've never seen before. It also says that she brings her food from afar. So I thought, *Okay, so she makes exotic dishes?* And the Lord said no, spiritually, she is like the merchant's ships. She carries the treasures of heaven within herself. She brings her food from afar. What is her food? The bread of the Word, the meat of the Word.

She brought her food from a distant place because she was alone with God in the secret place, and she brought it from the heavenly realm. Then she brought it out to the public and said, "This is what I got in the secret place. This is what heaven has downloaded into me, and you can have it too. I'm not looking for your money. I'm looking for you to be better than you came to me. I'm looking for you to be better when you leave me than how you came to me. I'm looking for you to be clothed in something different. I have a robe of righteousness that the Lord has given to me, and I have access by the power of the Holy Ghost, and you can have it too. We can fix you up. If you were in some dirty and filthy rags, let me tell you how to change your outfit. Let me tell you how to eat, if you're hungry. I've got something because I've been alone with Jesus in the secret place, in the distant place. I came away with Him and got alone with Him so that I could give you something that you need."

This is so good because you don't have to make anything. You don't have to make anyone a dress. You don't have to make anyone an exotic dinner. You just have to get alone with God and you can get the clothes and the food. But it's of a spiritual nature. Why? Because we don't have any ships. I was wondering how all of this stuff could apply to our lives because we don't seek wool and linen, we don't do merchant ships and pearls and rubies. But what we do have is flesh and spirit. We do have heavenly things. It's not so much about how well we work with our hands and if we're spending money on all the dresses or if we're clothing the whole community in fleshy things. He said to look at it from a spiritual perspective and see yourself.

Proverbs 31:15 says,

And she rises while it is still night And gives food to her household, And portions to her attendants.

I thought about a local ministry when I read this. It's called Rooted. This ministry was birthed from a desire in the heart of Abba for community and sisterhood among women in the kingdom of God. While meditating on this particular Scripture, I was thinking, *She rises up in the night.* I wasn't really thinking about midnight or morning, I was just thinking about the night seasons of our lives. Even when it's the darkest, I still have something to feed you. It doesn't matter if it's daytime or nighttime, the gospel works all the time. And when you're in the dark, you still have something for your family. Whenever you're going through hell in your life, you've still got something to take care of you with. And not only for your family, you've got something for your sisters. You don't have any maidens or servants, but you do have family, community, friends, and a Jesus family that God has given to you. So even in your night season, you have something to share with others. When you go into the commentary and read it, it says, "When she rises up in the morning while it's still nighttime, and the sun hasn't got up yet, and feeds her house." So once again, the Lord spoke to me and said, "Hey, Cody, I really need you to get up early and spend some time with Me so you have something to feed people."

Sometimes you make your kid breakfast in bed. May I submit to you that it's not just the breakfast in bed that you give them but it's when you wake up early in the morning and spend some time with Jesus, and you take them to school and you pray with them in the car on the way to school. You're feeding them and you're equipping them for their day. It's not just about children and moms, it's women. It's about reaching out to those around you and making sure they're okay, that you see people. Not just that you walk by and see them in the room, but you walk by them and you see your sister smiling, but you know on the inside that she's not, and that she needs a portion. That you need to pour into her and feed her something a little extra. You can see that the nourishment is being sucked out of her spirit, and you know that because you spend time with God. She might not have that right now, but you do, so you're going to give it. The more that we give, the more we are able to receive from Him. It's more blessed to give than to receive, so you give to others so you may receive more from Him so that you can be the conduit by which heaven gets into the earth and gets into someone else.

Proverbs 31:16 says,

She considers a field and buys it; From her earnings she plants a vineyard.

A few years ago, the Lord put this verse in my life and I didn't completely understand what God was doing or what He fully meant, and I've been praying about it. Does He mean actual land? As I began to dive into this, it means that she considered all the options and she said this is good, and she's going to sell out to it. She's going to buy in completely and totally. Going back to Matthew 13:44 (KJV), it says, "Again, the kingdom of heaven is like unto treasure hid in a field; the which when a man hath found, he hideth, and for joy thereof goeth and selleth all that he hath, and buyeth that field." So it's not necessarily that God is saying there's a field and He wants you to buy it. He is saying there is a kingdom plan for your life that He has specifically for you, and He needs you to see the treasure that's on the inside of that plan that's hidden away. He's going to need us to go sell out everything we've got in the flesh, to our fleshly ties. Sometimes God does ask us to sell our homes and our vehicles and to go out and do the work of the ministry, but sometimes He just asks us to sell out all of our earthly ties and all of our fleshly things and really buy into what He is saying for our lives. Consider the treasure that He has in your future, and what is in the plan of God for our lives, and sell everything else and buy into it. When you do, take the seeds that you gather from the land that He has given you and plant a vineyard, plant those seeds, and reproduce after your own kind.

What does that mean? Give Him souls for His hire. It's whenever we sell out to the kingdom plan and the field that He has designated us (which is the field of our lives), and we go in and dig up those treasures, and we get that precious seed out of the earth that's been buried, and we begin to plant it and see a harvest come up. He is the vine; why does He say plant a vineyard? It's because He is the vine and He wants to be in the center of everything that we do and He will produce the branches. He will bring the people and they will be connected to Him. And when we stand before Him one day, we won't stand there just saying, "Well, I got here." Instead we can stand before Him and say, "This is who I brought with me. These are who I sowed Jesus into. These are the stars that are going to go in the crowns that I'm going to cast at Your feet because You are worthy of it all." He has a plan, and in spite of what we thought, and in spite of how we worried about where the provision was going to come from, He doesn't need us to figure any of that out. He just needs us to see that there is a plan of God in our lives and then buy into it. He will take care of everything else. Buy into it and plant, reproduce, and see our fruit begin to multiply, and see our fruit remain.

Proverbs 31:17–19 says,

She surrounds her waist with strength And makes her arms strong. She senses that her profit is good; Her lamp does not go out at night. She stretches out her hands to the distaff, And her hands grasp the spindle.

I want to break down all of these Scriptures together. The King James Version says, "She girds her loins with strength." (I know I keep referring back to that particular version of the Bible, because it is the version I learned to memorize Scripture from. The NASB 1995 version is where I'm learning how to dive deeper.) I immediately thought about the full armor of God, where I'm girded about my loins with truth, that truth is the strength of my life, and that my loins are girded about with truth, because all of my reproductive organs are in my loin area. The seat of our emotions in Scripture and Hebrew culture is in the depth of your belly. Not in your heart, like we say here in America, but the seat of our emotions. And everything that we reproduce is in our loin area, the lower parts of our belly. And we're girding it with the truth of God and we're strengthened by His truth. We're protecting what is going to come out of us because we've got the truth of God wrapped around us. We're protecting our emotions and our mental health because we're not clothed with the lies of the enemy, we're clothed with the truth of the Word of God and what

He says about us. Everything that comes from us has to pass through truth to get into the earth. Everything that we feel has to pass through the filter of truth before it gets to stay, or it has to go. Truth becomes the discerning factor in our life, the standard by which we weigh everything. Is what you're hearing the truth or a lie? What's coming out of us is going to be protected.

"She senses that her profit is good." Not that I'm selling my wares, but that I have something to offer. I perceive about myself that what I have to offer is good. So many times as women, we think we don't have anything to give, or "mine is not as good as hers." It's not like that. You have to know and see that you have gifts, and you have treasures on the inside that God has given you. Your gifts have value, and your gifts are good. If your gifts weren't good, He wouldn't have put them in there. And if He put them in there, He means for them to go out. You have to see yourself for who you really are.

"Her lamp does not go out at night." You never stop shining. Not that you stay awake all night and get up early in the morning. It's no matter what season of your life that you're in, you never stop shining. The light of God never stops burning. We are always able to see Jesus, no matter what situation we're in, because we realize that we are called, and that we are fearfully and wonderfully made after the image of God. Our lives are a direct reflection of who He is, so we will shine.

"She stretches out her hands to the distaff, and her hands grasp the spindle." The spindle and distaff are a representation of the straight and narrow path. That she grabs ahold of the truth of God and grabs ahold of the strength of who He is, like grabbing the bull by the horns, and she holds on and does the thing. Even when she doesn't think she can. The truth that is wrapped around her says, "I can do all things through Christ which gives me strength." So I'm going to grab ahold of the straight and narrow way. I'm not going to get on the wide path because wide is the way and broad is the way that leads to destruction. I'm going to stay on that narrow way and hold onto the truth that I know, which is Him, and I'm going to be alright.

Proverbs 31:20 says,

She extends her hand to the poor, And she stretches out her hands to the needy.

This means that I'm always looking to see a need. I'm not living my life solely focused on myself, that I can only see me and mine, but I want to reach out and help. I will go above and beyond what is required of me. I will allow myself to be stretched and extended beyond my normal scope of reach because the need in front of me is greater and of more importance than the level of my comfort and security. Whether they are indeed poor in the natural and require physical comforts that I have been blessed with, or they are poor in spirit and need to draw from the wells of salvation, I have made myself available.

Proverbs 31:21 says,

She is not afraid of the snow for her household, For all her household are clothed with scarlet.

It's saying she's not afraid of the trials and tribulation or the storms that are going to come in her life because she has clothed her household with scarlet. Which means she has properly prepared the people around her to withstand the storm. That she's given her kids the tools they need to get ahold of God. She's told them where their help comes from, not just by telling them but by praying with them. She has shown them how to get to the secret place and how to get ahold of God. She has talked to her husband and clothed him and made sure that he was well taken care of, and she has wrapped him in prayer and bathed him in the blood of Jesus. She's pleaded the blood of Jesus over her family and self, friends, and the people that God has entrusted to her.

Proverbs 31:22 says,

She makes coverings for herself; Her clothing is fine linen and purple.

Coverings or tapestries, when you look it up, are bed linens. And I thought, *Okay, so we're making clothes out of bed sheets?* And the Lord said, "No, take it further." It's not about bed sheets, it's about what bed sheets represent: intimacy. She wraps herself, she makes coverings for herself, from the intimacy that she has had with the Father. She clothes herself in what she has gleaned from Him in the secret place. And her clothing is fine linen and purple.

Purple denotes royalty. She knows who she is and she knows that she is clothed with the intimacy that she has with her Father. She knows she is the daughter of a King. She is joint heir with Christ, and she is royalty in the Spirit. She is not a beggar, a peasant, or a maid servant. Though we be the servant to all and come to serve and not be served, we still know who we are.

Proverbs 31:23–25 says,

Her husband is known in the gates, When he sits among the elders of the land. She makes linen garments and sells them, And supplies belts to the tradesmen. Strength and dignity are her clothing, And she smiles at the future.

"Her husband is known in the gates, when he sits among the elders of the land." There are people who know me because of who I am married to. But since I've allowed God to do what He wants to, and I've gotten out of the box that the enemy had placed me in, and I've been doing the work of the kingdom, there are people who now know him because of me. It's not just that I'm known by him anymore, because I've let God do what He wants to do in my life. He's known by the works that I've been doing in the kingdom and outside of the walls of the building. When God has His perfect work in your life, it's a two-way street. Your husband gains favor with people because of the blessing and favor of God over your life. He doesn't just sit in those places because he sits there. He sits there because you encourage him to be the man that God has called him to be and it earns him a seat at the table. When you're speaking life into him, and you're speaking life into everyone else—and into yourself because you know who you are—it elevates everything around you. When God elevates you, it brings up the whole atmosphere of your home, your job, and everything else. People know where the blessing of God is coming from, and they see the value. There are people who have hired you because they know that the blessing and the favor of God falls on you, and if that's in their house or the facility where they make a living, they know they are going to be blessed just because you're there and because the favor of God rests upon you. If the favor of God rests upon you, it will rest upon the house. It's like the ark of the covenant.

Whenever David tried to bring the ark back from enemy territory, he brought it back the wrong way. The ark carried the blessing and the favor of God, so when he had to leave it at Obed Edom's house for three months until he could figure out how to get it all the way back to Jerusalem, Scripture says that Obed Edom's house began to flourish and prosper. Not because Obed Edom was all that, but because the covenant was in the house. You can bring the blessing and the favor wherever you are because the blessing is on you, because the ark of the covenant is inside of you. So wherever you go, His spirit is going. Even if you work for a heathen, the blessing of God works in any environment because it's not about them, it's about you being His kid. And He's going to take care of you and bless that place to prosper, because you're needing to get paid.

"She makes linen garments and sells them, and supplies belts to the tradesmen." She's giving to the people she's never met, to the people who are just passing through, because she's got an arsenal full of truth. The belt of truth. She's just passing it out. Anywhere she goes, she says anyone can have one. So when we meet somebody in the grocery store, on the street, or in the hair salon, you have something that you can leave that will last in their life. Just a little nugget of truth, just a little belt. We're not trying to dress them up from head to toe, but we can give them a place to start. If you can start with the truth, then everything can change. One little bit of truth can change a lifetime full of lies.

"Strength and dignity are her clothing, and she smiles at the future." This means that she is covered in strength and dignity. Arrayed in integrity of the highest degree. Her yes is yes, and her no is no. She rejoices in the time to come. She's not worried about how it's going to happen, she just knows that there's something great up ahead of her, and she's excited about it. She's not worried or fretting because she knows who she is. She knows who her Father is because she's spent enough time with Him to know that if He put that vision out there, He intends to fulfill it. Even if it doesn't look like what she thought, it's still going to be amazing. So I'm not going to look at my future and dread it. I'm going to look at my future and say, "This is it, and this is great." Everything He promises, He will do it. It will come to pass in due season, and in due time, He will make all things new. God does fulfill His promises, and they are good, and they are worth looking out into the future and saying, "Yes. You have my yes, Lord." I'm not going to worry about the doubt or the fear or the worry. Just yes. He's got me, and I've got Him. I'm just going to be happy and full of joy because you know what? I don't have time for any of that other stuff. We've wasted so much time being afraid, depressed, oppressed, or whatever you have felt, that you just have to say, "You know what? I'm done," and choose life, joy, and peace.

Proverbs 31:26 says,

She opens her mouth in wisdom, And the teaching of kindness is on her tongue.

We don't speak like crazy ladies on the warpath. We speak the wisdom of God. We don't give petty advice to people saying, "Well, I know he did that. You know what I would do?" If you have that attitude and it's coming out of your mouth, that's not the wisdom of God. That is the flesh, and you need to stop talking. The wisdom of God is first gentle and peaceable. You can give advice even if it's hard, and it will come with peace and you won't have an attitude about it. We're looking for something bathed in the Holy Spirit. Not saying you can't be feisty or a warrior, but you can't have that petty attitude. A petty attitude doesn't become a warrior. A warrior keeps their peace and keeps their head and their emotions. Why? Because if not, they will get their head cut off. When you start playing into all the petty stuff, that's when you lose your focus and the enemy is allowed to get into your mind, and if he can get into your mind, then he's got you. So stay out of that place.

Proverbs 31:27 says,

She watches over the activities of her household, And does not eat the bread of idleness.

She makes sure that she knows what is in her home. A woman knows. There's something that God has given us on the inside, that we know. We may not know what, but we know when something isn't right. And when you have your home, you can go and cleanse that home and pray over it, asking God to show you where this is in my house. If it's something physical, take me and let me put my hands on it and get it out of here. You know the company that is in your home. You know if the company is of heaven. You know if the peace of God is in your home. You know if all of the demonic forces of hell are in it. You have the authority to get it out. You don't sit idly by and let hell take over your house. You don't just sit back and wish it would get better some day. You take your stance, and you stand against the enemy. You don't fight against your husband, children, friends, flesh and blood; instead, you go to war with the enemy of hell that is trying to come against what's yours.

Proverbs 31:28–29 says,

Her children rise up and bless her; Her husband also, and he praises her, saying: "Many daughters have done nobly, but you excel them all."

There's a lot of good women in the world, but if you're going to excel and go exceedingly and abundantly above, it's only going to be because Christ is living in you. Christ is within you, you will not fail. People can do good things, but without Christ it's never going to go beyond that. All things are possible with Jesus.

"Favor is deceitful." This means charm is deceitful. You can be lying while being charming to people. Beauty is fleeting. Don't be so focused on how well you talk to people and how pretty you are. Talk is cheap. But the virtue and the morals and standards that are on the inside of us, the Lord has already told us, is far above the most valuable pearl. It's worth everything. Beauty fades. Everything that is up is going to go down. It's the law of gravity. Don't put all your energy into something that is going to go down. Focus on what's on the inside.

Proverbs 31:30–31 says,

Charm is deceitful and beauty is vain, but a woman who fears the LORD, she shall be praised. Give her of the product of her hands, And let her works praise her in the gates.

It's not that you are never going to receive a pat on the back from people, but what you do for God will stand alone and speak for itself. You don't have to beg for people to accept you or to be on your team or side, but what you do for God will speak. It will not lie; it will tell the truth every time. The trail of blessings and testimonies that you leave behind you and around you will be the proof of who you are and who's within you. It will tell your motives. It will tell everything. The work will tell the story.

A lot of you are already the Proverbs 31 woman, you just might not have realized it yet. I challenge you to make a list of the things you do, all of the great things in your life—things you do for others, things you like about yourself—and see who you really are. See that there is more about you that is already like the Proverbs 31 woman than you think. Be free from striving to become some lady who works 24 hours a day and never misses a beat. You will never attain this. Be the woman of God that you were born to be! Be full of vision, purpose, passion, and the Holy Ghost. Maintain your relationship with the Lord and keep growing. Hear Him when He speaks, see what He shows you through His Word, and share that with your husband, children, friends, community, and even strangers. You are responsible for your obedience to Him and what He asks of you to do, not everyone else's ideas or interpretations. Seek to please Him first, above all else, and you will not be found wanting.

CHAPTER FOUR

A Divine Reflection

W OMAN, WHO ARE you? The Bible says you are a reflection of Him. Not just a regular image either. You are a divine reflection of Him on the earth.

Second Corinthians 3:18 says,

But we all, with unveiled faces, looking as in a mirror at the glory of the Lord, are being transformed into the same image from glory to glory, just as from the Lord, the Spirit.

"We all." All of us. Everyone is included. Everyone that the Lord calls, everyone that He draws. Every woman, every man, every child, they are all called to this one place, beholding the glory of the Lord. We are changed, we are transformed, into the same image from glory to glory even as by the Spirit of the Lord. So we see that it's all inclusive.

"With open face" means that we have been unveiled, and when you look it up, what that word really means is that everything that hindered me no longer hinders me. I can truly see Him for who He really is. I don't have a misconstrued idea of who God is because of how He's been misrepresented to me by people who have claimed that they are from God, but they are really operating in the flesh. All of my flaws, and all of my sin, and all of my failure that caused me to be separated from Him because I didn't understand that He loved me past those things, and that I am worthy of His love—all of that has been removed, and I believe that's something God has been doing steadily in this book. He is breaking down our walls, breaking down the things that hinder us from being in right standing and right relationship with Him.

Everything that's hindering us from going boldly to the throne room of grace so that we can find help in the time of need, God is tearing down brick by brick, stone by stone. He is making a way. There are no stumbling blocks to get to Him anymore because He has removed those. We are transformed into the same image that we see in that mirror. Whenever we look, we don't see ourselves anymore. When we look ahead, we see Him. We see His reflection. The more we serve Him, the more we go away with Him, the more we have intimacy with Him, then the more of Him begins to be deposited in us. The more of us leaves and the more of Him comes in, and then the more of Him we see in the mirror.

The Scripture says that we are transformed into that same image that we see. We are transformed into the image of Christ from glory to glory. And as I looked that up, it said that *glory* in the New Testament means opinion, and it's always good. We are changed from one opinion to the next opinion in a good way. We walk out of old things and we are transformed into what He says and to His good word over our lives. It also means praise, honor, and glory from one divine quality. That's what I love the most. From one divine quality that we have acquired from Christ, to another divine quality that He adds to us. All the time, He's steadily changing me. He's steadily taking things out. The Lord will prune us, and when He prunes us, the things that He takes off are gone. So He takes away little pieces of us that don't need to be there so that He can give us a divine quality that is like Himself, so that we begin to appear as He appears, and we begin to be a reflection of Him in the earth.

When Scripture says that our faces were unveiled and we beheld His glory, I thought about Moses and how he came down from the mountain, and the glory of the Lord showed so much on his face. His face was so bright that they asked him to cover it because they couldn't stand to look at him. They couldn't understand the level of what was going on. But the Lord said in the New Testament that once Jesus has come and the Holy Spirit has come, once the church has been born, He said take the veil off of your face and let the whole world see the light of His goodness. Let the whole world see His glory. Don't be hindered from seeing Him because of your sin and your shame. He died to get rid of it. And also don't let anyone else be hindered from seeing Him.

Don't ever dumb down anymore. Don't ever dull your shine, because your shine is His shine. You know, our shine isn't our shine anymore. We shine because He shines in us, and we are to bring the light into the darkness that is this world.

In John 4:23–24, we read about where Jesus met the woman at the well, and He says that the time is come, and now is, whenever the true worshippers will worship God. They won't worship on this mountain, but they'll worship everywhere. We're not going to worship in the confines of religion or the confines of the law; we're going to worship in spirit and in truth. For God is a spirit, and they that worship Him must worship Him in spirit and in truth.

So, as the Lord said, we have taken Proverbs 31 and we have taken Titus 2, and as God has begun to teach it to us (or reteach it to us, because several of us have heard these things our whole lives), He's beginning to take it out of a physical realm and into a spiritual realm.

If we're going to be transferred from glory to glory, you have to realize that the transfer from the flesh to the spirit was made when Jesus came into the earth. The Old Testament was all about the law. It dealt with the outward sin and what man was doing. But Jesus told this woman that there was a shift coming. They wouldn't be doing worship that way anymore. The time has come and it now is. Why is the time now? Because Christ is here. The time and the season has shifted because His feet have touched the earth. So you've got to get out of the form and the fashion, and you've got to step into the realm of the spirit. We can be transferred from glory to glory. Not just in the physical, but we're transformed in the spiritual because Jesus understood that it was going to take a spiritual remedy. The problems that were going on weren't just that people were killing each other, because that was just the action, that was just the fruit. The law never dealt with the root of the issue, it always dealt with what the real issue produced. The law killed.

Second Corinthians 3:4–6 says,

Such is the confidence we have toward God through Christ. Not that we are adequate in ourselves so as to consider anything as having come from ourselves, but our adequacy is from God, who also made us adequate as servants of a new covenant, not of the letter but of the Spirit; for the letter kills, but the Spirit gives life.

Jesus came to make a transfer out of the flesh, out of the Old Testament, which always dealt with the carnality of men and women. And He said He wants us to walk in the Spirit because the letter will kill us, but the Spirit will bring us life. We may say, "Well, how does that happen? How does the letter kill but the Spirit brings life?"

Let us look to Romans 8:1–4. I know this doesn't seem like it's about women, but I'm telling you, once we understand what's happening here, it's all going to connect. Everything that the Lord's been doing is going to be tied together. This passage says,

Therefore there is now no condemnation at all for those who are in Christ Jesus. For the law of the Spirit of life in Christ Jesus has set you free from the law of sin and of death. For what the Law could not do, weak as it was through the flesh, God did: sending His own Son in the likeness of sinful flesh and as an offering for sin, He condemned sin in the flesh, so that the requirement of the Law might be fulfilled in us who do not walk according to the flesh but according to the Spirit.

"What the Law could not do, weak as it was through the flesh." The law had no provision to deal with the heart of man. It was weak through the flesh, because the flesh always deals with what it sees with its eyes. That's what the Lord said when Samuel went to anoint David as king. He said, "Look, I know you're thinking it's the tall brother. I know you think it's the good looking brother. But man sees on the outside and I see in the heart and what's going on in the inside." So, we see a type and shadow of where we're headed eventually, and that God is going to make a better way because He said He created something that people are only looking for on the outside. But when He sends Jesus, everything is going to transform and we're going to begin to look on the inside and not just what we see in the natural.

"The law of the spirit of life" through the Son in Christ Jesus who came in the likeness of sinful flesh. And that means He came in the likeness of you and me. He looked like us. He looked like He had the potential to sin, but He never did. He came in the likeness of sinful flesh for sin, and He condemned sin and death by the sacrifice at Calvary and through the spirit of life. We are able to receive life through the Spirit because of what Jesus did. The spirit goes into the heart. For example, the law said if you commit adultery, you will be stoned. But Jesus came and said if you look at a man or woman, and you do it in your mind, you're already guilty. Why? Because it's not about the sin, it's about where it starts. It's about the renewing of your mind. He said that we are renewed in our mind because we can't think like the flesh, we have to walk in the Spirit. We have to be renewed in Christ in our mind so that when we look at women, and we look at men, we're not having thoughts about how "fine" they are. We are instead thinking, *God, what do You want to say to that person?* Lust has to leave, because lust isn't the action. Lust is going on in our minds before the lust is ever played out in a bedroom somewhere. Murder is played out in the mind before the gun is ever drawn. He said even when we're talking about people, we're murdering them. So it's a heart thing and a spirit thing. Once we get our spirit and the inside right, we don't have to worry about the law, because the law is fulfilled whenever we walk after the Spirit and not after the flesh. If we're walking in the spirit, we're not talking about people, we're not after somebody else's husband, we're not fulfilling the lusts of the flesh because we can't walk in both at the same time. So Jesus said if you're going to look like Him, you're going to have to let Him transform you, and you're going to have to walk in a new way, in a new mindset, and in newness of life.

Romans 8:5–6 says,

For those who are in accord with the flesh set their mind on the things of the flesh, but those who are in accord with the Spirit, the things of the Spirit. For the mind set on the flesh is death, but the mind set on the Spirit is life and peace.

When we walk in the spirit, we're not concerned about what she did or what she said, because we've got bigger things going on. We're looking at Jesus. We're looking at where we're headed. We're not looking at where we've been or what we've been through. To be carnally minded is death. The flesh always brings death; it always brings condemnation. When we get out of the spirit and we start walking in the flesh, we stop seeing who God has called us to be and we start seeing all of our shortcomings. We begin to magnify them and we begin to make them greater than the blood of Jesus, who died to cleanse us, free us, and redeem us from those things.

When you start to get down on yourself, check yourself. Are you walking in the spirit? He said there is no condemnation to them which are in Christ Jesus who walk not after the flesh, but after the spirit. If you're feeling the condemnation and the daggers, and you're feeling unworthy and ashamed, check that. That's flesh talk, that's not spirit talk. The spirit brings life. I'm not talking about conviction. Conviction says, "We're going to trim this off so that you can be better in this area." He's not mad at us, but He's going to trim that part of us and move on. Whereas condemnation says, "You're doing this and God's never going to use you again because you're awful and terrible." That's not Jesus, that's not the Spirit, so shut that down, get back up, and follow Him.

The carnal mind is enmity, or at war, with God. The flesh is always at war with what the Spirit of God is saying, "because it is not subject to the law of God, neither indeed can it be so then they that are in the flesh, cannot please God." We see here that the flesh and the Spirit are always warring against one another. The Lord brought this to my remembrance. He said, "Remember whenever I told My disciples the temple will be torn down and will be raised in three days, and like me, I'm going to be torn down and in three days I will rise again? And Peter said, 'No, Lord. No, no, no, that's not going to be.'" This was in Peter's carnal mind, even though he was right next to Jesus all the time and he was hearing His words.

There are times that if we're not careful, we'll step out of that. We'll start thinking about spiritual things in fleshly ways and we will say, "No, Jesus, that's not the plan for Your life." Jesus then turned around and said, "Get behind me, Satan," because what Peter said was contrary to what God had spoken over His life. He knows what God has said over His life, so He was saying to Peter, "Don't you dare put on your fleshly mind and call down what God has ordained through the spirit to take place in My life, because you don't realize that what God is going to do in My life is going to save your life, Peter, and the lives of all those who come after you. So I come against you."

I know this person, and they said this one time, that if we're not careful, we can operate in the flesh. In the sanctuary, in the world, we can operate in the flesh if we're not careful. There are gifts of God, there is prophecy, there is edification, there are words of wisdom and of knowledge, but if we're not careful, we won't speak the words of God. We will speak what we think about the situation, instead. I know someone who was getting a "word," and the word they were receiving was contrary to everything that was going on in their life. This person knew that the enemy wasn't the person that was delivering the word, but it was the spirit in which they were operating. So the person hearing the word withstood the person speaking it and said, "I don't receive any word that you just spoke over me in the name of Jesus."

Jesus realized that Peter was the one to whom He said, "Upon this rock I will build my church and the gates of hell will not prevail against it." Not because He was building it on Peter, but He was building it upon the relationship. That when people know who He is, and He knows who they are, there's nothing in hell that can stand against what He will do in those kinds of people. He knew that was going to take place, but He also knew that at that moment, Peter was not operating in the spirit of God. He was operating in the carnality of his mind.

So we don't come against the person, but we come against that spirit they're operating in. Jesus did it, and we can too. Don't get mad at the human being, be mad at what they are allowing to work in them to try to turn you from what God is saying over your life. You don't have to receive every word if it's totally off the wall and if it's contrary to everything that God has been speaking to your life. You cast that mess down. You say, "I don't receive that in the name of Jesus. I love you as a person, but I don't receive that in Jesus' name because that doesn't line up with anything that God has been speaking to me." There are times when things need to be withstood face to face, and there are times when God will tell you not to receive something. Don't think every time that you have to say it out loud to the person giving you the word.

Peter needed to know God knew the potential in him. Jesus knew the potential of him, and what he was going to do, which was to preach to 3,000 and see them get saved. And He couldn't have Peter operating like he was. If He was going to use Peter the way He wanted to, He had to correct him. So if you feel that rise up in you, and you feel like that's what you need to say, then you can say that. And if you feel like you just need to tell the Lord that you don't receive that, and that word has no authority over your life in Jesus' name, then you follow the Spirit of God as you are led by Him.

Romans 8:8–12 says,

And those who are in the flesh cannot please God. However, you are not in the flesh but in the Spirit, if indeed the Spirit of God dwells in you. But if anyone does not have the Spirit of Christ, he does not belong to Him. If Christ is in you, though the body is dead because of sin, yet the spirit is alive because of righteousness. But if the Spirit of Him who raised Jesus from the dead dwells in you, He who raised Christ Jesus from the dead will also give life to your mortal bodies through His Spirit who dwells in you. So then, brothers and sisters, we are under obligation, not to the flesh, to live according to the flesh . . .

How do I put to death the deeds of the flesh through the Spirit? You keep surrendering to the Spirit of God, and let Him have His way in your life. When He needs to take something out or deal with it, like gossiping, let Him deal with it and take it out. The quicker we surrender to Him as He brings things up to us, the faster we're going to move forward in the kingdom. We need to stop waiting on God, because He's waiting on us to surrender everything. Our person doesn't like it, and it hurts sometimes, because we don't think that we are capable, or that we can let go, but we can do all things through Christ who gives us strength. He's never going to say "let Me have that" and not give us the grace and the strength to do what He's asking us to do, to walk in what He's asked us to do. So we mortify the deeds of the body through the spirit, because when the spirit has its way, the spirit deals with the roots, and if the root is dead, then the fruit is dead. The deeds of the flesh are killed because God has killed the root of the issue, because it's always birthed on the inside. Murder isn't birthed on the outside; murder is birthed in the heart. The Spirit is dealing with the things of the spirit; therefore, when those things are healed, there's nothing to throw a stone at anymore. The law throws stones, the law kills, but the spirit brings life. Where the fruit of sin and the fruit of the deeds of the flesh used to be, now there's fruit of the Spirit, and you can't throw a rock at that.

Roman 8:13–17 says,

For if you are living in accord with the flesh, you are going to die; but if by the Spirit you are putting to death the deeds of the body, you will live. For all who are being led by the Spirit of God, these are the sons and daughters of God. For you have not received a spirit of slavery leading to fear again, but you have received a spirit of adoption as sons and daughters by which we cry out, "Abba! Father!" The Spirit Himself testifies with our spirit that we are children of God, and if children, heirs also, heirs of God and fellow heirs with Christ, if indeed we suffer with Him so that we may also be glorified with Him.

Whatever you do in your life, it's going to reflect Christ. If you're going to be a woman of God, Christ is going to be seen in you because you're going to allow Him to have His way in you. I want us to see clearly the transition from the flesh to the spirit, and that Jesus came to get us out of the fleshly realm and into the spiritual realm. When the New Testament talks about Christ, it also talks about the first Adam, which is the Adam in Genesis. The father of creation, which came through Adam. The first Adam was fleshy, but the last Adam, which is Christ Jesus, is spirit. The first Adam failed in the garden and in sin. But the last Adam came and was victorious and did away with sin. God has said in prior

Scriptures that He saw it was not good that men should be alone, so He created a helpmate, and this is where we get the term *ezer*. In Genesis 2:21–23, it talks about how God caused a deep sleep to go over Adam, and I know we have already covered this, but I wanted us to go back so we could clearly see one to the next. God opened him up and took a rib from his side and He created woman.

At Calvary, in John 19:34 while Jesus is hanging on the cross and He is giving His life, the Bible says that He was already dead, and the soldiers were coming around to break the legs of the accused as was customary during crucifixion. When they broke their legs, it would help kill them more quickly. But it had been prophesied over Jesus that not a bone in His body would be broken, so when Jesus cried out, "It is finished," He gave up the ghost and He went ahead and died. The other two were still alive beside Him, so the soldiers went to them and broke their legs. They went to Jesus and saw that He was dead. They didn't break His bones because there was no point in it. The soldiers took their next move, which may have been done out of spite, but which God allowed with His intentions in mind. God permitted what was next for a purpose. They took a spear and pierced Jesus in His side, and the Bible says that blood and water began to flow out of His wound.

Here we now see that as woman was taken out of the rib of man, the church—His bride—was born at the cross. He was pierced in His side, blood and water began to flow from His side, and the church was born in the baptism of the Spirit, which is the water, and she was born of the Spirit because the blood had done away with all of sin. The blood was the atonement, the blood was the sacrifice, the blood was the remission of the sin that would keep her bound in the flesh. And the water was the pathway into the spirit because God said He is taking His people out of the fleshly realm by the blood of the Lamb, and He is moving them into the spirit by the Holy Ghost that began to pour out of the side of Jesus. Born of the spirit, and born of the blood. Born into the newness of life, and upon that is our foundation—that we have a remission for our sins and an atonement for the debt that we owe because of the sin that we committed. We owe it no longer when we accept His blood into our life. When we accept that blood, we also receive the Spirit of God into our life, who becomes our teacher and becomes the one that opens our understanding of the Word of God and says, "Look at what the Word wants to tell you today."

The more I thought about it, I was like, *Oh man, Jesus said He's in the Father, the Father's in Him, and He's sending us a comforter, who is going to testify of Christ. What does that mean?* It means that Christ reflects God, God is in Christ, and the Holy Spirit is going to reflect Christ, and Christ is going to reflect the Father. He's not going to testify of Himself. We come not to testify of ourselves, we come to testify of who He is and what He's done. And that's how Christ gets into the earth. That's how people see Him in us, because we're not talking about us, we're talking about Him. We may tell our story, but it's not so people learn about us, it's so people can learn what He can do for them, because of what He did for you.

In Proverbs 31 and Titus 2, it says that we are a direct reflection of Christ in women. That she will do good and not evil all the days of her life, she seeks wool and linen, works willingly with her hands, she is like the merchant's ships bringing her food from afar, she still has food even when it's dark. Jesus said He is the bread of life; if any of His children ask bread of Him, will He give them a stone or a serpent? Absolutely not. He's going to give you everything you have need of. And when I see this woman in Proverbs 31 and she's feeding others, we are talking about how we're not just feeding our family, we're feeding everyone that God surrounds us with. Not with our physical food. Sometimes it's physical food, but a lot of the time, it's that spiritual impartation that He has given to us in that secret place, and we're giving it to others. That's Christ. That's Jehovah Jireh being reflected in our life. When we lay hands on the sick and we see them recover, that's a reflection of Jehovah Rapha, the Lord who heals me. Whenever we begin to love people and we begin to cover them, that is Jehovah Nissi, the Lord my banner, His banner over me is love.

When we extend that covering instead of condemnation, when we reach our hands to the poor, that is everything that Jesus did while He was here. He said if our enemy is hungry, feed them. If somebody is naked, clothe them. If they need water, even if you give them a sip of water, do it in His name, and when you've done it to the least of these, you've done it unto Him. He said if somebody is walking and they are weary, go a mile with them, and don't just go one mile with them, go with them two. I immediately began to think of the two men on the road to Emmaus. They were talking about Jesus and how He was crucified and what they were going to do, and Jesus walked with them. He walked with them not just for a little bit, He walked with them all the way to their house, until they got the realization that this is who He said He is. We are Christ in disguise in the world. When you walk out, the Christ within you is dressed up, and it might look like yourself, but it's Christ. It's the Christ in you, the hope of glory.

If we're ever going to understand who we are, we are going to have to have an unhindered view of who He is, so that we can be transformed from one divine quality to the next divine quality, because Jesus said we are fellow heirs with Him. That means that we're not trying to be so far above Him that we can't be reached, but we're right there, we're joint heirs. We were birthed from His side. Just as woman was birthed from the side of man not to be walked on, not to be lorded over, but to be equal and to walk together. We see this church was born of His side. Why? Because He's making us joint heirs to get His mission and His kingdom out in the earth. He said He's not going to make you below Him, and He's not going to make you above Him, but He's going to make us suitable to walk alongside Him because He's going to deposit who He is into us and bring us up to sit in heavenly realms. Where we were abiding in a fleshly realm, He's going to bring us up in the Spirit. Not that we are little gods or anything, because that's not what this is. This is that Christ has given us power and authority, and He has called us to sit with Him in heavenly places, that He has given us a seat at His table, and that He has put so much of Himself on the inside of us, not to give ourselves glory or to boast, but to say look what He did in us.

The enemy will say, "Look what you've done. You will never be anything." But Christ says, "Look what I've done so that you CAN be all that I have intended for you to become." He will say, "Look what I gave you! I took that mess and I turned it around, and I made it not to look like sin and death anymore, but I've made it look like Me. I've dressed it in My righteousness. There's no good thing that I've withheld from you."

Matthew 25:40 says,

"And the King will answer and say to them, 'Truly I say to you, to the extent that you did it for one of the least of these brothers or sisters of Mine, you did it for Me.'"

Like the Titus 2 woman, we're not gossiping, we're not slanderers, we're not murderers with our mouths, but we're the ones who reach out like Jesus would. We say, "You know what, I know you've been found in sin, but I don't condemn you. Go and sin no more." We're not going to tear anyone down but instead love them through it. Love them OUT of it! So when people have issues, like the woman with the issue of blood, we're not studying the issue, but we're speaking life into them. That healing can come, and the virtue can come, and the dead can be raised, because the same power that raised Jesus from the dead is the same power that works in us.

I've said it from the beginning, sometimes we just don't realize what's coming out of our mouths until later. For us to ever correctly understand anything, we've got to understand who He is. Through the mirror of Scripture, we can really see Him and what He does, how He loves us, how He's powerful, and how He will fight and kill the enemies who come against us. He's also strong enough and humble enough to come down to where we are and love us. The same hand that kills the enemy in our life is the same hand that lifts us up and draws us to His breast and tells us that we're okay. That He's got us. That He's our covering. He is strong, and He's gentle. He is providing for us and going ahead of us, but He's not just going ahead of us where we can't see Him anymore. He's going to walk us there until we get to where He's already been.

I'm so excited about where God is taking us, and that we're understanding that the more we know about Him, the more we really know about ourselves and who we are. We are a divine reflection of Him in the earth. We were created to show forth His character to those around us and to shout His praises and His fame for all of our days.

CHAPTER FIVE

The Ezer

W<small>E WILL BE</small> talking about the woman as "The Ezer" in this chapter. This is literally the chapter I have wanted to get to for this whole book. It is the inspiration that this book, this study, this revelation was birthed from.

Genesis 2:18 says,

Then the LORD God said, "It is not good for the man to be alone; I will make him a helper suitable for him."

When you look at the literal translation of this passage, it says, "The Lord said it is not good that man be separated, or that man be apart, or that man be alone. I will create for him, I will form for him a help meet." That word *help* is ezer, and that means the first line of defense, the one who goes out in front of. The *meet* means a helper, a front line worker, someone that comes alongside who is suitable, or compatible, or comparable to himself. So when God created woman, He didn't create woman to be a slave or to be beneath, but He created woman to come alongside of, to come out in front of. He formed her from the rib of man, and we talked about how the church was born out of the pierced side of Jesus at the cross with the blood and the water. We see woman formed from his rib because she is a helper. She is not beneath him, she is not behind him, she is actually out in front of him. She is, in essence, the first line of defense for the home, the first line of defense against the enemy that would try to come in. The rib is a protector for every vital organ in the body that man needs to survive.

Proverbs 31 talks about how she looks well to the ways of her house; she does not eat the bread of idleness. When we went through Proverbs 31, we talked about how women aren't just here to keep the house clean and to wash the clothes and to wash the dishes. Yes, you do have to do those things, you're not exempt; but it's not always just the natural things that we're to be doing. There is a spiritual work we are to be doing. That women know what's going on in the home, women are more in tune with the spirit, and with the spirit realm more naturally because that's how God designed us from the beginning. Men are great, men are wonderful, we love men, and we respect men in their authority in the home. God did create them to be protectors, to be the covering, to be the provider, and all those are all aspects of God's character that He has given to men. But an aspect of God's character that He has given to women is the ezer.

I want to take us in Scripture to the first mention of the Lord's name being Ebenezer. In 1 Samuel 7, we see the Lord is calling Israel to go out to war with the Philistines and to care for the ark of the covenant. In verses 7–12, their preparation time for battle, it says,

> *Now when the Philistines heard that the sons of Israel had gathered at Mizpah, the governors of the Philistines went up against Israel. And when the sons of Israel heard about it, they were afraid of the Philistines. So the sons of Israel said to Samuel, "Do not stop crying out to the LORD our God for us, that He will save us from the hand of the Philistines!" Samuel took a nursing lamb and offered it as a whole burnt offering to the LORD; and Samuel cried out to the LORD for Israel, and the LORD answered him. Now Samuel was offering up the burnt offering, and the Philistines advanced to battle Israel. But the LORD thundered with a great thunder on that day against the Philistines and confused them, so that they were struck down before Israel. And the men of Israel came out of Mizpah and pursued the Philistines, and killed them as far as below Bethcar. Then Samuel took a stone and placed it between Mizpah and Shen, and named it Ebenezer, saying, "So far the LORD helped us."*

In the name Ebenezer, the *ezer* is at the end. So *eben* is the stone and *ezer* is the help. The Lord is the stone of our help. He is our rock, He is our fortress, He is our mighty strong tower where unto we continually resort, and He is our ezer. Why? Because He went out in front of us. Except before, when the Philistines came before Israel, they could not do anything. They said they were scared. They needed help, and they asked Samuel to call on the name of the Lord. And Samuel called on the name of the Lord. Samuel made a sacrifice and God heard him. The Bible says that the Lord showed up in great thunderings and He confused them. So the thunder that went before Israel when they went into battle actually helped to discombobulate the enemy. It shook their brains and their understanding. They didn't know what was happening to them, and it allowed Israel to come in strong and to finish what God had started.

So we see God coming out here as the first line of defense, and He always did. We see several instances of Him going before them into battle and confusing the enemy and messing them all up. Sometimes He would have the angels just slay the enemy completely. But in this particular case, in reference to the Ezer, He came out with great thunderings, and He confused the enemy so badly that Israel was able to come in and utterly destroy the Philistines. So it's God's personal character that He has given to us as women, that we sometimes go out before our family, or that we go out before our husband knows what's happening, before anybody else knows what's happening, and we're already fighting battles in the spirit before anybody else sees what's going on. We're already winning stuff before it even hits our kids because we know it's coming from a distance. We don't just cower back and shy away, but we go out to meet the enemies coming against us and those we love.

The Lord has given me several women that I want to highlight in this chapter. Every woman in the Scripture that God uses for good are women of God. A lot of times, people want to focus on the Esthers, the ones that humble themselves and look pretty and get the job done. Or focus on the Ruths because Ruth is quiet, gleaning in the field, and laying at the feet of Boaz. Those are the kinds of women that the world wants us to be, and there is nothing wrong with that. But all women are not quiet and sitting at the feet of men. Some women are loud, and they're boisterous, and they are not afraid or timid, and they just go for things. And if we're not careful, then religion will try to put you in this box and tell you that if you're not Ruth, or you're not Naomi, or you're not Mary sitting quietly at the feet of Jesus and weeping and washing His feet with your tears or drying them with your hair, or you're not beautiful Esther making fancy dinners or quietly making your requests known to the king, then you're not what God wants—or you're a raging Jezebel and you're just trying to take over the world. That's just not true. If you are a woman who is a Ruth, or an Esther, or a Mary just quietly serving your King, there's nothing wrong with you. Absolutely nothing. Please hear my heart and don't take this chapter and think you're all wrong. No, I want you to know that God created each and every woman for the purpose He created her for. We need the Ruths, we need the Esthers, we need the Marys, we need all of those people to do what God would have us to do. We need the Marthas that are going to prepare ahead and make sure everything is taken care of, and I will get to all of that in this chapter.

But for now, I want to bring hope to those who question where they fit into this kingdom, because maybe your personality does not look like it matches what everybody is saying or wanting. Maybe your gift seems a little out of place or out of order, or time, or season. I just want to speak life and hope into you, that if you're a loud girl, if you're a go-getter, and if you're a leader, it's okay. Women lead in this kingdom. He created us by design in the beginning to go in front of. Just like Judah always went out, and the praisers always went out before the battle was won, He created us in that same sense. We are the ezer, we are the helpmeet. We're not beneath in a way that we're supposed to be walked on; we're under the covering of our husbands, but we are not under his feet. We are the first line of defense. We are, at times, pretty, quiet, and subtle. But we are also fierce, we are warriors, and we are capable of leading in unity with those that God has joined us with.

Let's begin in Judges 4. We see here that God has raised up a woman, and her name is Deborah. Judges 4:4 says,

Now Deborah, a prophetess, the wife of Lappidoth, was judging Israel at that time.

In the time of the judges, Israel was not under a kingship because the Lord wanted to be their King. We do not see Israel getting a king until 1 Samuel. But from creation all the way up until the kings stepped in, Israel was governed by God, who had given the law to Moses. So judges had been set up throughout Israel to help lead the people, and the judges under God at that time were the highest authority in the kingdom and to the nation of Israel. If there were a physical king, it would have been them. But they were not called kings, they were called judges. Deborah is a judge. She is a woman. She is a female and she sits in the highest seat of authority in the nation of Israel. It's okay for a woman to lead, because God put a woman in leadership. He didn't just say that she was a judge, He also said she was a prophetess, one who hears from God, one who sees what's going on in the spirit realm, one who can call things that are not as though they are. A warrior. Unashamed. Unafraid. She was not just one thing.

That's what I hope that you can see out of this the most. You can be more than just one thing. You are more than a cookie cutter, one-size-fits-all woman, and that is OKAY! It's on purpose, even. Some of us feel like we have about 50,000 personalities, and it's not that you have multiple personalities, it's that you have multiple gifts because God has created you to be full and well rounded. There are some days where you walk in one gift more than the other, but it's because you're filled with the Holy Spirit. Whenever you get saved and you ask Jesus to come into your heart, Jesus saves you, but the Holy Spirit comes in as your teacher and as your guide. And when you're filled with the Holy Spirit, you're capable of being used in any of the gifts of the Spirit at any given moment, as God seems fit or deems necessary. So one day, you might be a little more prophetic, one day you might be a little more intercessor, one day you might be preacher, or evangelist, or whatever God needs you to be in that moment—because you've been bought by the blood of Jesus, you're not your own anymore, the Spirit is within you, and whatever God wants to do with you, He will.

Going back to Judges 4 . . . God puts Deborah in a leadership position. During this time, there was a man that had been tormenting the children of Israel for something like 20 years, and it was time for the reign of terror to come to an end. Judges 4:1–4 says,

> *Then the sons of Israel again did evil in the sight of the LORD, after Ehud died. So the LORD sold them into the hand of Jabin king of Canaan, who reigned in Hazor; and the commander of his army was Sisera, who lived in Harosheth-hagoyim. The sons of Israel cried out to the LORD; for he had nine hundred iron chariots, and he oppressed the sons of Israel severely for twenty years. Now Deborah, a prophetess, the wife of Lappidoth, was judging Israel at that time.*

In the face of all of this oppression, Deborah finds herself saying, "You know what? I've had enough, and I believe the Lord has had enough, and I believe the people have had enough. So I am going to go out before the army of Sisera, that is underneath this king, and God is going to send me help, and we are going to be done with this because I'm over it." There comes a point in time in our lives where we see what the enemy has done, and how he's been doing it for years and years. He's been attacking your families for years. He's subtly come in until he's grown into a great force, and you don't see any way that he can be overcome. Tap into the Holy Spirit and be woman enough to say that enough is enough, and we're not doing this anymore. Pray to God and ask Him when the right time and season is, and when He lets you know that, step into what He has for you.

When she began to step out and say, "We're going to begin to come against Sisera because this is ridiculous. His army is just tormenting everyone around me," the Bible says that Barak rose up and came alongside Deborah. It didn't say that Barak was already above her and that she had to rise up to him, but that she was above him and he had to rise up to her. Barak came and joined himself to her. When you step out in the authority that God has given you, God will bring people alongside you, and He will bring them to help you accomplish the mission He has set for your life. I see it a lot in my church, that men of God are rising up. Why? Because I'm not trying to be some crazy lady telling the men they need to bow down to everything that I say. But God is saying He wants there to be a balance. When there's a mighty female presence, there must be a mighty male presence. In the beginning He created male and He created female. And He wanted them to walk together in the spirit of unity and make the kingdom known in the earth. So I see it that God is not only raising up women in the church, but He is raising up men to come alongside us and say that they see the vision, let's do what we need to do to make it accomplished in the earth. So Barak comes alongside her, and he does what he's supposed to do to accomplish the mission.

I want to go to Judges 4:17 where it says:

Now Sisera fled on foot to the tent of Jael the wife of Heber the Kenite, because there was peace between Jabin the king of Hazor and the house of Heber the Kenite.

If you continue reading from verse 4 down through verse 17, you will see they're in the middle of a battle, and Barak's army is destroying Sisera's army, so Sisera deserts his post and he flees. One of the customs of that time was not to just destroy the army but to find their leader, hang him and kill him, and to bring his head so they can display it on the city wall. Then they can make everybody passing by be afraid and know they are not to be messed with. So Sisera had fled and they were wondering what they should do. In Judges 4:15–16 it says,

And the LORD routed Sisera and all his chariots and all his army with the edge of the sword before Barak; and Sisera got down from his chariot and fled on foot. But Barak pursued the chariots and the army as far as Harosheth-hagoyim, and all the army of Sisera fell by the edge of the sword; not even one was left.

Then going back to verse 17, we read that Sisera was going to a place where he felt like there was going to be peace, but God had placed a woman in the house of a man who had made an alliance with the king of Canaan. Sisera thought when he went to that tent, that he was going to be safe. Don't ever underestimate the power of an ezer who has been hidden in plain sight by God in the middle of enemy territory.

Judges 4:18–21 says,

And Jael went out to meet Sisera, and said to him, "Turn aside, my master, turn aside to me! Do not be afraid." So he turned aside to her into the tent, and she covered him with a rug. And he said to her, "Please give me a little water to drink, for I am thirsty." So she opened a leather bottle of milk and gave him a drink; then she covered him. And he said to her, "Stand in the doorway of the tent, and it shall be if anyone comes and inquires of you, and says, 'Is there anyone here?' that you shall say, 'No.'" But Jael, Heber's wife, took a tent peg and a hammer in her hand, and went secretly to him and drove the peg into his temple, and it went through into the ground; for he was sound asleep and exhausted. So he died.

You are a warrior! Don't let anyone mistake your hospitality or sweetness for weakness. God will use your gift to lure in the enemy, and you will kill him, you will strike him in the temple, and you will nail him to the ground. The place where the enemy feels like he is the safest, he is not out of reach of God—or out of the reach of people God has placed in position. God has placed you in the setting you are in strategically for such a time as this, to destroy the works of the enemy. To come against the hand of the enemy that is against the kingdom of God, your family, your brothers and sisters in Christ, your church, the land, and the region. You are where you are on purpose, so do what God says and know that you can be sweet and precious, but you can also kill the enemy and nail him to the ground. Don't ever let the enemy come in without nailing him to the ground, and also don't forget that the enemy is not flesh and blood, but he is masquerading around hiding behind people's faces. When you want to retaliate against people or hurt people, recognize that it's not them, it's the spirit that's using them and that they're allowing it to use them, to come against you. Kill the enemy, not the people.

I want to talk about several people from the passage in Romans 16. This is the last chapter in the book of Romans. Everything that is happening throughout Romans, when Paul sends out a lot of writings about leading the church, he's more or less giving them a course on how to get their stuff together, how to run the church, what they need to do, and what they don't need to do. But when we get to Romans 16:1, the last thing he says is,

> *I recommend to you our sister Phoebe, who is a servant of the church which is at Cenchrea.*

When he says, "I recommend to you Phoebe," it means he wants to commend, he wants to establish Phoebe, he wants to stand near Phoebe, as his sister, as his fellow laborer, who is a servant of the church. A servant of the church means that she is

an administrator. A lot of people want to call Phoebe a deaconess. Phoebe was not a deaconess; she was a pastor, she was an administrator of the church of God, she served the church of God,
she served Paul and the ministry, and she was pastor of a home
church in Cenchrea, which is in Corinth. They call her a deaconess because a deaconess sounds better to some people than a
woman as a pastor. Certain religious groups and cultures would
let her be a deacon, but they would not let her be a preacher or an
apostle, because she was a girl, and they were men. But we now
know better.

The kingdom of God is as much for the daughters as it is for
the sons. There were just as many women that walked with Jesus
as there were men. There were just as many women that were a
part of the ministry as there were men. Yes, there were 12 disciples, but it wouldn't be very appropriate for the Son of God to be
sleeping in the same area at night time with a bunch of women.
So it's not that Jesus didn't want women to be involved. Women
were involved everywhere they went during the day and everywhere they went that they were ministering. But as far as who He
was going to sleep in proximity to at night, or who He was going
to lay His head next to, it would have been very inappropriate for
a single man to be living in the same facility as a single woman,
and He would never bring offense to the ministry. So He picked
the men God wanted Him to pick and did what God wanted Him
to do.

But He did not leave women out on where the church was heading. He did not leave women out of the resurrection. He did not leave women out of preaching the gospel, of carrying the Word of God, or of serving the church in any capacity that a man can serve in. I do want you to know that you're not above a man. Don't try to take authority over a man by force, that's not scriptural. You don't have to go and fight for your place in this kingdom anymore. You are free! Men do not have to fight for their place and we don't have to fight for our place. Why? Because we are all the sons and daughters of the Most High God. It's not that man is trying to have the rule over you, or that you're trying to have the rule over man. The struggle for power has been one of the most effective tools ever launched against the human race since the birth of the church and the death of the apostles. We must fall in line with the whole counsel of the Word of God.

If you're a married woman, your husband needs to be your covering, he needs to be surrendered to God, and he needs to be walking in the right path. If He's not, you trust in God, that He will be your shield and your covering until your husband fully submits and surrenders, because God will not leave you naked and unprotected when you're trying to be obedient to His Word. You're not trying to rule over your husband, but you are trying to do your job. And your job as the ezer of your home is to be the first line of defense. To make sure that nothing gets in the gate of your home, nothing gets in the portal, nothing gets through your TV, or your cell phones, the front door, or the back door, the laundry chute, or from any crevice of your home that's not from God. And if it does, you ask God to help you sniff it out, let you find it, and get rid of it. Be that first line of defense for your church, be that intercessor, be the one that speaks up when you see something happening.

If you have a word for your church, go to your pastor and ask if you can speak it to them, or maybe it's just a word for your pastor. Be subject to whatever that authority tells you to do, and do not get offended if you are told to wait. Do whatever God says in whatever capacity that He says. Make sure you stay in decency and in order as much as possible, because some people are going to make it as hard as they can for you, but God will make a way. You'll only hit a brick wall for so long, and then God will bust that wall down, let you go free, and He will move you into a place where you can operate and do what you have been called to do.

So, Phoebe is a servant of the church which is at Cenchrea. I know I keep saying that, but I want it to sink in. We also know that Paul wrote the book of Corinthians to the church at Corinth, but Cenchrea is also in Corinth. And guess where Cenchrea is? It's in the port city of Corinth. A port city is a city of exchanges. It's where the ships are coming in and where they're going out. It is the first line of defense to get into Corinth. God led Paul to set a woman at the gate of exchange where goods are coming in and goods are going out. He said to set a woman there, because she's going to be nosey. She's going to want to know what's on those ships, what they're bringing in, and what they're doing. See, people think we're being nosey to be rude, but God created us to be that way. He created us to be investigative. He created us to ask questions and not just to settle for what the answer is on the surface. Why? Because we need to find out what the hidden agenda of the enemy is. Not just because Phoebe was trying to be up in everyone's business, but that she needed to know if there was anything in those ships that could have caused harm to the city, because if there was, they could just take it and put it back on the ship and take it back to where it came from. Phoebe is the ezer at Corinth. She was at the first line of defense for Corinth because she was positioned at Cenchrea.

The Bible says in Romans 16:2,

That you receive her in the Lord in a manner worthy of the saints, and that you help her in whatever matter she may have need of you; for she herself has also been a helper of many, and of myself as well.

Paul is basically saying, "You honor her, you help her. If she calls on you or needs you, or whatever she asks you, you better do it. Because she has been a help not just to other people, but she has been a personal help to me. And you receive her like you receive me." So Paul was saying people may have felt like she was lower than him, but he was bringing her up to where he was at.

Romans 16:3–4 says,

Greet Prisca and Aquila, my fellow workers in Christ Jesus, who risked their own necks for my life, to whom not only do I give thanks, but also all the churches of the Gentiles.

Priscilla (Prisca) and Aquila are a husband and wife team, and they're missionaries with Paul. They are also pastors of a home church. More times than not, you are going to see Priscilla mentioned before Aquila, which is not normally customary because we always want to mention the husband first, and then we'll mention the wife. Paul sometimes says Aquila first then Priscilla, but most often when you see them mentioned in the Scripture, he says, "Greet Priscilla and Aquila." Why? Because she is just as vital to the ministry as he is. She is just as much a part of what God is doing in the earth as he is. We're not going to belittle Aquila, we're not going to forget him, and we're not going to put him in a corner and act like he doesn't exist. But we also will not stand for her to be put in the shadows and act like her contribution to the kingdom of God does not matter.

Ladies, what you do matters. If you see someone doing something for the kingdom of God, be like Paul and tell them. Tell them that you commend them and thank them for what they're doing for the kingdom of God and how they're seeing through the vision, because sometimes people just need to know that they are seen.

Romans 16:5–7 says,

Also greet the church that is in their house. Greet Epaenetus, my
beloved, who is the first convert to Christ in Asia. Greet Mary,
who has worked hard for you. Greet Andronicus and Junia, my
kinsfolk and my fellow prisoners, who are outstanding in the
view of the apostles, who also were in Christ before me.

Andronicus and Junia—two names that are not well known
in most of the Christian community. In fact, this is the only time
that Junia is ever mentioned in the Scripture, and until around
the 2000s, in the Scriptures, it said, "Andronicus and Junias."
Somebody added an "s" to the end of her name. Whether that
was by human error or it was by trying to keep ladies out of important leadership roles, it doesn't matter. But they found out that
Junias wasn't a man. Junia was a woman, and she was an apostle.
Paul said she was his fellow prisoner, his fellow laborer, and that
she needed to be greeted because she was an apostle in Christ before him. Which means what? That they go out before him? That
they do the work of the ministry? That they believed Christ before Paul saw Him on the Damascus Road? That they caught the
vision before he did? That she saw Christ for herself? That Christ
called her? We don't necessarily know. Some questions will stay
unanswered for now. But why try and blot out her existence to the
rest of the world? I would never call myself a prophet, or call myself anything for that matter. I am not searching for a title or to be
known. At the end of the day, I just want to call myself His.

There are times in your life where you know that there is an anointing of a prophet on your life, that there is an anointing of a pastor or an evangelist, or whatever the case may be. But I have always known that there has been an apostolic anointing on my life, and I have always shied away from it because all I had ever heard from the outside world (not the church I grew up in) was that women could not be apostles. So if people ask you to show them where it says it's okay for women to be apostles, show them Junia. There's only one verse about her in the Bible, but that is all you need to know. And just know that if it was possible then, it's still possible now. I tried to fight that for so long because we tend to make ourselves feel like a Jezebel, or we're walking in this wrong spirit, or that you bowed down to wrong teaching and the devil's trying to use you. It makes you second guess what God is trying to do in your life, but from here on out, know who you are.

Woman, who are you? All you women of God who are called to more of the front line, leadership positions, who have always had a struggle in the back of your minds about if you're really supposed to be doing that. You know what people say, but you really have this feeling that it's the call on your life. You just don't know what to do with it. You question yourself about if you should obey God, or if you should obey man, and how you fit into this kingdom. I started preaching when I was a young kid, and I would go and do revivals. And one time, I was at a church and there were these two older gentlemen there. I was a little teenage girl, about ninety pounds, and the guys were big, gray headed, old men of God. And they said to me, "Well, you'll be a really good youth leader one day. You'll be able to speak and preach to women." And I thought, *No, I'm going to preach to everybody. I love kids, old people, and everybody in between. I love people. I'm going to preach to all the people. I'm going to tell anybody that will listen that God has a plan for their lives. Red, yellow, black, white, pink, purple, man, woman, girl, boy, I don't care.* Even from the very beginning of the launching of my ministry, there have always been people that just come and attack that. Finally I just had to tell myself, "I don't think this is what y'all have been saying that this is. I think this is what y'all have been taught." And even now, to this day, there are still people who ask others if they are really going to sit under a woman pastor. God makes those, so yes, people are going to sit under a woman pastor and evangelist. There are even people who say that apostles don't even exist anymore, and I don't even want to fight that. I just know that there is an anointing, and when it's in the earth, it never leaves the earth. People may die and people go out, but their mantle, the anointing, it never diminishes or dies out. Elijah and Elisha are a great example. Elijah left here, but the mantle remained. The anointing, when it is in the earth, never leaves the earth.

There are mantles that are laying all over this earth waiting for somebody to pick them up. The anointing that was on your grandmother, that was on the people five generations back from you, is still on the earth. The day that Billy Graham died, I was on my way to the post office, and as I was driving I said, "God, who's going to walk in that mantle?" He said, "I'm ripping that mantle and I'm dispersing it because it's too much for one person to carry." He said, "I'm going to give a little here, and a little there, to whosoever will reach for it." At that moment, driving past the Piggly Wiggly in Chipley, Florida, I reached up in my car and just grabbed it down and by faith, grabbed a piece of that anointing, because once it's here, it never leaves.

So from when the apostles walked the earth, the mantles that they carried are still here today. They were crucified upside down. They were boiled in hot oil. There were all kinds of things that happened to them. We may not be a literal "apostle" because we have not seen Jesus Christ in the flesh, but that apostolic anointing is still in the earth, and I can walk underneath that apostolic anointing whosoever that I am. Jesus didn't say, "Whosoever will, let them come and be saved, and invite them into the kingdom of God," to just say, "Well, you can do it, but you can't." No, whosoever means whosoever. Whosoever can be saved, and whosoever can do the work of the ministry. If your life is lined up with the Word of God, and you are living in accordance, in full surrender, and full obedience to Christ Jesus, you can walk in whatever the Lord says you can walk in. Now we can't walk in something that isn't ours. We can't go to someone else's church and just say we're going to be the pastor now. That's not our area or our lane. But we can go and support someone else's church and their pastors. Let His glory be made known.

There are enough churches that if everyone were to get saved, and we stop worrying about building a church and start worrying about building a people, every church would be full. We need to get on the kingdom page and see what God is really trying to do in the earth, that it's not a battle between men and women, because He created us in the beginning to walk in unity. But the enemy has driven a wedge over a struggle for power that God never intended. He didn't birth a marriage for a man and a woman to be in conflict with one another all the time. He created us to be in unity, to walk together in peace, and to do the work that we are supposed to do to build a family, populate the earth, to be in unity in marriage and in the home.

We can't work together as churches because the enemy is driving a wedge and making us argue saying, "We don't do it like you do it, and I just don't like that." It doesn't matter what we like. That's our preference, that's how we interpret it. What do we agree on? That Jesus came, that He died, then He rose again, and that He came to seek and to save that which was lost. If we can't get together on our doctrine or on our interpretations, let's at least get together on this and let God sort out the rest. There is so much conflict when there shouldn't be. All of these little divisions. If we could just get to the root of what the enemy is trying to do in our churches. Because he will destroy it if we let him.

Ladies, whatever church you go to, if you start hearing gossip— people talking about people—pull out that wedge! Speak up and say that the enemy is not going to come in and destroy your church. Don't allow that to come into the body. If you see it, cut it off to the root. Tell that person that you love them, but that they're allowing the enemy to use them to tear down something that they need to keep their mouths off of, and pray with them. You are the first line of defense for your church. You can't just expect your pastor to handle every single thing. If you see the enemy sneaking in, it's your job to squash it. You can kill the snakes that are coming around the perimeter. You can be the first line of defense.

Romans 16:8–13 says,

Greet Ampliatus, my beloved in the Lord. Greet Urbanus, our fellow worker in Christ, and Stachys my beloved. Greet Apelles, the approved in Christ. Greet those who are of the household of Aristobulus. Greet Herodion, my kinsman. Greet those of the household of Narcissus, who are in the Lord. Greet Tryphaena and Tryphosa, workers in the Lord. Greet Persis the beloved, who has worked hard in the Lord. Greet Rufus, a choice man in the Lord, also his mother and mine.

We may not know everyone that he is calling out, like Rufus' mother, but their works speak louder than their name. That has always been my prayer: "God, may the work I do for You be greater than my name."

Romans 16:14–16 says,

Greet Asyncritus, Phlegon, Hermes, Patrobas, Hermas, and the brothers and sisters with them. Greet Philologus and Julia, Nereus and his sister, and Olympas, and all the saints who are with them. Greet one another with a holy kiss. All the churches of Christ greet you.

Making sure these people were greeted meant that Paul commended them. They were worthy of praise and honor. And in this list we see that there are almost just as many women as there are men. Maybe not all mentioned by name, but all the men weren't mentioned by name either. It was said to greet them and the brothers and sisters who were with them. Everybody was treated the same. Everybody was given equal honor, and everybody was together. Women being the ezers on the front lines of ministry and a kingdom work that was spreading to the uttermost parts of the world. When will we ever get back to the simplicity of spreading the good news? To reach a world that is lost and dying in their sin, it is going to take all hands on deck. To make disciples will require male and female hands that are willing to leave the struggle for power and jump into the trenches and walk with people once again. We must care about the people more than we care about the power.

No one can take away who God has made you to be. If they never recognize your gifts or the anointing you carry, it changes nothing. People do not make or break you. Scripture tells us that it is to our own master that we stand or fall. Never forget that above all else, you live to please an audience of One. Take your position, daughter of Zion. Whether you are a Mary, Ruth, or Esther or you are a Deborah, Jael, or Junia. We NEED all of you being the ezer you've been created to be in the space that God positioned you to occupy. Get out of the box that you have been shut up in for all this time! Fight the good fight for those you love and those you've never met yet, who are hanging in the balance. Night is coming and there is no more time to waste. Let's be all we can be while we still have a chance.

CHAPTER SIX

The Contender

WOMEN ARE EVERYWHERE in the gospel. They're everywhere in the building of the kingdom. Everywhere that there is a man of God, there is a woman of God as well, coming alongside, helping, leading the way, the front line of defense, in prayer, in fasting, in preaching the gospel, prophesying over people's lives—and that is doing the work of the ministry. It's not a one-sided thing, but it's an "us" thing. I want to utilize the King James Version of Philippians 4:1–3. It says,

> *Therefore, my brethren dearly beloved and longed for, my joy and crown, so stand fast in the Lord, my dearly beloved. I beseech Euodias, and beseech Syntyche, that they be of the same mind in the Lord. And I intreat thee also, true yokefellow, help those women which laboured with me in the gospel, with*

Clement also, and with other my fellowlabourers, whose names are in the book of life.

I want to stop there because in verse 2, we see two different names. "I beseech Euodias, and beseech Syntyche, that they be of the same mind in the Lord." Both of these people are women. They were two women of God that were active in the church of Philippi and in the growing of it. It doesn't necessarily say what their jobs were, but I wanted to point this out because we've been pointing out so many positive things about women in ministry. And I want to point out something that is very real: if we're not careful, and we don't labor together in love, then the enemy will come in and cause division. Euodias and Syntyche were both working for the same cause, in the same church, with the same mission, but they had different ideas on how to approach doing what needed to be done. And because both of them were strong women, neither one of them wanted to give. I want to point out how important it is to be unified in the body of Christ, to be unified with those that we are working with. Not just in our churches, but in the body itself, and in the kingdom, because we're all on the same team.

There are several churches that are being represented everywhere, and it's very important that we see we are all out for the same mission, and that mission is to see lost souls be saved, to see those who are bound set free, and to see those who are hopeless be encouraged and know that they have a lively hope, and that it's not a dead hope, and to see the gospel be preached to the world to the whosoever will. Paul said he wants us to be of the same mind. And to be of the same mind sometimes that means we have to give and take. Sometimes that means that we have to humble ourselves to someone else and say, "Your idea is better, let's go with that." We don't always have to be right. Now, we may feel like we've heard from God, and they may feel like they've heard from God, but somebody is going to have to give so that the enemy doesn't take a good thing and turn it into a bad thing.

If you are in a church, you obviously have some sort of leadership. You have pastors, associate pastors, teachers, elders, deacons. Every place is different in how they set up their leadership. Whenever God speaks to your leadership, you need to submit yourself to that. It's very important to understand this, because if we don't know, or haven't been taught these things, then we will allow the enemy to come in and tear down a lot of things, when God doesn't want it to be that way. He wants to build it in unity, He wants to bless unity, and bless people being together, and not us being driven apart by our own ideas, or what we think we heard, or what we think we thought. So if your pastor or your leadership tell you the vision of their church, or how they feel the Lord is leading them, but you have some other idea, it doesn't mean that your idea isn't great; it just means that your idea may not be for right now. You need to pray about it, and you need to submit yourself to the vision of that leadership. If you can't come into agreement with that leadership, and if you feel like what they're saying is wrong, you need to pray for your leaders. You don't need to tell everyone around you, you need to quietly take it to the Lord and ask Him to help you see, or help them see, whoever's eyes need to be opened. We always need to go into prayer not just thinking that the other person's wrong and not us, because as human beings, that's so easy to do. Instead, let's go into our prayer closet, and let's say, "Lord, whoever needs to see more correctly, help them see." And it's not necessarily that you're wrong, or they're wrong, but sometimes you just may not be in the right field yet, or in the right place yet. Your vision may not match the vision of the place that you're going. And if it doesn't, that's okay. It doesn't mean that your church is wrong, and it doesn't mean that you're wrong; it just might mean that God's doing something else, and you need to follow what God's doing in your life. After you pray, submit it to the Lord and to God and say, "Lord, where does what You've given to me fit in? Is this something You're asking me personally to do, or is this something that You want the whole body to do?"

Sometimes we want to take the personal things that God's telling us to do, and we want everybody to do our part. So sometimes when we get in our prayer closet, we should ask God things like, "Is this an 'us' thing or is this a 'me' thing? Am I trying to make it an 'us' thing when You're making it a 'me' thing?" And He'll show you. But I would say to you, just submit to your leadership. Go with what God is telling them. He set leaders in place on purpose for purpose. Do people in leadership always get it right? No, because they're people, and they miss things, and they'll get it corrected if you'll pray for them and not bash them, and if you'll be patient and let God do what He wants to do. And if God doesn't change them in the prayer, maybe God will be changing you.

I have personally been on both sides of it. I've been in the congregation when I've thought to myself, *This is not it.* So I know what it feels like to be so passionate about how you know what God is speaking to you, but you're seeing something in front of you that is so different. You just need to pray about it. Just like the Lord was patient with you and getting your life together, and as God has walked with you getting your stuff together, He will do for them also. God has placed those people in leadership there on purpose. He wants them to do good, He wants to use them for the kingdom of God and His great purpose, so He's going to give them a space to get their stuff together. You may not be able to endure all the grace that He wants to give them, and you may want to tuck tail and run, but you need to deal with that before the Lord, and you need to submit yourself and keep your mouth closed. Don't gossip. Don't be slanderous and get into those prayer meetings where it's really a gossip session. Pray earnestly to the Lord. Ask God about yourself first, then pray for them and cover them. You don't know what they're dealing with, and they don't know what you're dealing with unless the Lord tells them.

So we just need to stand in the gap and pray for each other, and contend to keep the faith, and keep the unity in the spirit through the bonds of peace. And if it's time to move, it's time to move. If it's time to stand firm, then stand firm. But you'll only know that by prayer. You won't know that by your emotions, because there are many times where your emotions will tell you to run, but your faith will keep standing, and God will orchestrate it where He will deliver you. One day it will be like that, and the next day it won't be like that anymore, because God works all things together for good to those who love God and to those who are called according to His purpose. Whatever He does in your life, it's going to be good—good for where you came from, good for where you're going, and good for not only you but also for everyone involved. God's going to work it all out for good. That's the first thing that He said to us, saying, "Women of God, I need you to be women of God. I need you to maintain, and I need you to keep the unity. Be in the same mind and of one accord because that's where my blessing comes down."

"And I intreat thee also, my true yokefellow, help those women who labored with me in the gospel." Those women are the nameless women in the gospel, and that's not uncommon. There are a lot of women in the Bible who are nameless. We know their location and what they did, but we still have no idea what their names are. But God does, and that's what He's saying. "Help those women which labored with me in the gospel, with Clement also and with my other fellow laborers whose names are in the book of life." Because the things that we do for God, we don't do them so that people will know our name. We do them so that His name will be great in the earth. As long as my name gets into the book of life, I don't care if it's published in any other book on the planet.

Our names are written in the book when we are saved by the blood of Jesus. That matters. But there's so many times in our life that we think that if somebody doesn't recognize us, or if somebody can't see us/our name, that it doesn't matter. Yet everything that we do for His name, every time we give a glass of water, every time we sweep a nasty floor, every time we wipe a baby's bottom in the nursery, every time we do any little, tiny thing for God, whether people say thank you, whether they notice or not, your name is written in the book of life, and the book of remembrance is also a part of that. He said, "Every time you even mention My name, every time you think about My name, I'm writing it down." So if He's a God that notices not just the acts that we do with our hands, feet, and our mouth, but He is a God that recognizes what goes on in our head and in our heart, that's all that matters.

Paul is speaking to all of those women—and maybe he's like some of us, knowing if we start mentioning names, we will forget people that we didn't intend to forget, so we just say "everybody who helped" or "you know who you are." That's kind of what Paul is doing here. He's saying, "I just need y'all to know that these women helped me, and I want you to come alongside them and I want you to help them. I want you to help the yokefellow." He said, "Help my true yokefellow, my companions, my colleagues. I want you to help those women."

Help in this passage literally means to assist, apprehend, seize, and become pregnant. I thought, *What!? You want us to help those women become pregnant?* Sounds absurd, so I didn't stop there. I kept on the trail, and this is where is led me: He's saying, "If you are a companion of mine, if you're a colleague of mine, if you're somebody that says you come alongside me in the faith, I want you to reach out to these women and I want you to assist them. I want you to apprehend them. I want you to grab ahold of them and say, 'I'm with you.' I want you to seize them." Seizing is like apprehending, but it's very intense. It's a pulling to yourself. It's not just keeping people at arm's distance. How many times do we do that in the kingdom of God?

God says, "These are My people," and we're "saying" we love them and we are for them, but only from over here. Here in my comfort zone. God is calling us to love up close. Stop loving from a distance with arms outstretched. Get in the same field, get in the same room, get in the same call, get in the same mission, and do this thing together. He said, "I want you to help these women. I want you to seize them. Apprehend them. Assist them." And now for the wildcard: "become pregnant with them." It's time that we become pregnant with the vision of the kingdom of God! Not our own little things that we have going on. Yes, we all have little parts and pieces of the puzzle, but the overall vision of the kingdom, the overall work, we need to have a passion, we need to have an intimacy with God that births that in our bellies! That we carry the purpose of God in our hearts so that it would be birthed into the earth.

He said, "Those women who labored." *Those that labored* means those who strove with me for the cause of the gospel, who cooperated vigorously, who shared my struggle, who competed together with me. They did not compete against me. They competed with me and believed in what we were doing. Because who are we competing against? Not you and me. Not flesh and blood. We are competing against the enemy. Help those who competed with me, who struggled with me. Those who, when I was going through hard times, weren't just sitting there lollygagging, sitting around, and talking about me and the mission. They were the ones holding babies, cooking meals, praying in the secret place, and standing in the gap. They were contending WITH me. If I was getting stripes, they were getting stripes. If I was in agony, they were in agony. Maybe they didn't do it physically, but they were holding me up, they were fasting for me, and when I was away in other places, they were carrying on with the work of the gospel.

Paul was an apostle. He was going from town to town and he was leaving behind this group of people to stay and continue the work while he was away. Do the work of the ministry. That's why we have the letters to the Philippians, the Corinthians, the Ephesians, the Galatians, the Colossians, and all of these different places. We have these letters because he's speaking and communicating back to the people that he had left behind to continue in the work. Paul didn't just leave men to do the work. He left men and women. And apparently there's a lot of women that are doing the work, so quit being crazy and help them. In that day, and in that time, as per their culture, women and men were supposed to be separated. Women were uneducated. Women didn't get all of the luxuries that men got. And because it was easier, they wanted to stay stuck in their culture and they wanted to stay stuck in their traditions. Paul told them they cannot.

They cannot refrain themselves from those women. They needed their help. They were doing the work of the ministry, so they needed assistance. It's high time that we come out of culturalism, and the "this is just our way and this is how we do things in the south and this is how we do things in America." Paul was saying, "Hey, everybody, let's just help everybody." Jesus was surrounded by women; Jesus was surrounded by men. It didn't matter if it wasn't customary for all of them to be together all the time, and women were over here, men were over there. We find Mary sitting at the feet of Jesus in a room full of men. We find Martha cooking for all of them.

The kingdom of God comes, to be the kingdom of God. He doesn't adapt to our culture, we adapt to His. I was thinking about what Paul said in the New Testament. He said when he's with the Romans, he's a Roman. When he's with the Greeks, he becomes a Greek. When he's with the Jews, he's a Jew. Whenever he's with the lawless ones, he said he's like the lawless, except for he obeyed the law. He hung out with them, and he talked with them, and he talked like them, but he didn't offend God. He didn't come against the law of God in any way. Why? What is the reason? Because he just might win some.

He meets people where they are. We adapt ourselves to fit the culture, not so that we can stay in that culture, but so we can reach somebody where they are. There are places in my area, in my region, that I cannot minister because in their church culture, "I" don't make sense. So when I go, I keep my mouth shut, and I'll blend in. I don't act haughty or force others to recognize me or the call on my life, because God recognizes me. I just go with the flow of how they operate. I respect the authority of the house and what's going on there. Why? Because they may not agree that God called me to preach, pastor, or even speak to crowds of mixed company in any capacity, and they may not agree that I'm capable of doing what God said, but I'm not going to disrespect them. How is disrespect ever going to make people see? It's not going to help. I don't need any other human being's approval to validate the call on my life—and neither do you, friend. We don't have to defend it, justify it, or debate it. He is our defense. Be respectful and let the fruit speak for itself. Let peace be your position.

At the church I go to, we wear pants. We wear whatever, as long as you cover yourself up and don't have your business hanging out everywhere on purpose. When I go to other churches, they wear dresses. When you get behind the pulpit, you wear a dress. That's just the way certain people grew up. So when I go there, I don't wear pants because that's disrespectful. When you try to go out and evangelize, you know the places that do like what you do, or that understand it the way that you understand it. Just be respectful. It's not a heaven or hell issue. There are places you don't know how they believe, so what will it hurt to walk in with a skirt or a dress on? It won't hurt a thing. You're not being a hypocrite. You are simply adapting yourself so that the gospel might be preached. We must realize that there's something bigger than us going on. There's something bigger than what the law of the tradition of that time said. Paul realized it, and thus he said, "I'll become like they are so that I might win some."

Jesus came and He broke the mold. He said, "Yes, she can. Yes, he can. Yes, they can together, and I'm going to be the glue that pulls back into place what God designed from the beginning to be together, that man has caused to be separated." We talked about how the enemy turned gender into a power struggle when God created male and female in the garden. God created them to be one flesh. He created them to come alongside one another, being in unity, and they were—until the enemy came in and made that power struggle over who would be the boss and would have the most control over the other. It's not about who's telling who what to do. It's about this: My husband is my covering. I come under the covering of the man that God has placed in my life and has joined me with. We don't fight for power. We submit to one another, as Christ loved the church and submitted Himself and gave Himself for the church. Women, submit yourselves to your own husband. It's a mutual submission. It's not a power struggle. It's unity.

Christ came to bring everybody together. They all sat under the same roof. They all sat at His feet. Whenever He was preaching off the boat and they sat in the field, they all sat together. It was just the kingdom of God. It wasn't about all the things that people make it to be. They cooperated with each other vigorously. They shared with each other in their struggle, they competed with each other, together in the gospel.

A dear friend of mine sent me Philippians 4:3 out of the NIV translation, and it says this:

> Yes, and I ask you, my true companion, help these women since they have contended at my side in the cause of the gospel, along with Clement and the rest of my co-workers, whose names are in the book of life.

When she had sent it to me, *contend* is the word that stuck out to me the most. It doesn't say contend in the KJV. *Contending* here means to labor, cooperate vigorously, share my struggle, and compete together with me. All of these words go together and tie in to make up a contender. The writer is saying, "Those women who contended with me." A contender is someone who competes as an individual or a group in competition or a campaign in order to win or achieve something.

No one of sound mind ever goes into a fight unless they have the ability to win. We wouldn't pick two people off the street and say, "You're going to box." There are weight limits and restrictions that have to be met if you're going to have a legitimate battle. They would need to weigh in because they've got to be evenly matched by size. You can't put a 200-pound girl against a 98-pound girl. That's not a fair fight. She doesn't have a chance of winning. If she's going to be a contender, you have to find somebody else who's around 90–105 pounds and pair them together, because they have a shot at having a really great fight. Realizing this, it makes the fact that he said that she was a contender so much more powerful. It's like God saying, "You have a chance to win in this thing! I haven't placed you in something that's above your head. I haven't placed you in something that you're not capable of being successful at. I haven't placed you in an area or in a part of the body that you can't succeed in."

"She contended with me." When you break that word down, if you look it up in the dictionary, the Latin says it's *contendere*. *Con* means "with" and *tendere* means "stretch and strive." A contender is someone who is stretching with. Someone who is striving with me, not against me. They're for me. They're on my team. When we read that part of the Scripture, we can see it as "stretching with me." Stretching is the place that I believe the Lord is wanting us to get to.

He said, "The women that are going to be reading this book, I'm stretching them. I'm calling them out of their comfort zones. I'm asking them to stretch with me. Don't just do what you've always done." I know this is kind of different for a book, but I do feel like it's very prophetic in the teaching and it's going to be very on-point for where you're at in your life. Some of you reading this, you have been in a holding pattern. Loving Jesus, praying, asking God, etc. And some of you are beginning to stretch. However, He wants to do even more in your life, so He is about to stretch you again. You're about to do things that you never thought you could do. You're about to see things in the spirit you never thought you would see. Things are going to come out of your mouth and you're about to see answers come to pass. When you pray, the Lord is going to move and bring those prayers to fruition on the earth. He says, "You are a contender. You are a woman who is contending in the faith with Me."

Paul is dead and gone, a man with whom we don't contend with anymore. But right now, we are contending with Christ for the victory of the kingdom in the earth. The fulfillment of what God wanted to take place from the very beginning is happening in this time and in this season and you are a part of that process. You get to see what that plan is going to look like. So He is saying, "I want you to stretch with Me."

I want to go to Isaiah 54, and this is going to go along with Chapter 5, when we were in Judges 4 and we were learning about the battle with Sisera and Jabin, and how Deborah had risen up. God had raised up a judge in Israel that wanted to see God's people delivered from this king that had had them bound for a long, long time. So God raised her up and He raised up Barak to come alongside and fight with her—or her fight with him, vice versa, however you want to look at it. But she called him out and she said, "God has already told you what to do and here I am to confirm it. Now, let's go and do the work." Barak said, "Well, if you'll go with me then I'll go." So they go up and they do the work. They fight the battle, and the enemy starts being overcome. Then Sisera, the captain of the host, goes into the tent of Heber and he thinks he's going to find refuge, because Heber has broken with the Kenites and has destroyed the unity that the Kenites had with Israel. So he's broken the loyalty between his people and Israel. He's come outside of that room and he has joined himself with Jabin and Sisera. Jael is the only one in the tent at this time, and he comes. She invites him to come into her tent and to rest a while. He says, "Can I have some water?" And she said she would get him some milk while he went to lay down. He lays down, drinks some milk, and then in just a minute, the Bible says that she took a tent peg from her tent and she drove it through the temple of his head and she killed him.

So God used this woman in a mighty way to take the head of the enemy that was a plague to the people of Israel. Fun fact: back in those days, women were the ones who set up the tent. Women literally came before their husband, while their husbands were out doing other things, and they would set the tent. So the tent that she had set up one million times before, the stake that she had driven into the ground one million times before, God was preparing her for this one battle with the enemy. Taking those things that she thought were so dumb, for this one moment in time, and the enemy was destroyed, and the Israelites were free from this evil that had overtaken them for all these years.

So what you're doing may feel like it's mundane and you feel like it doesn't matter, but it is what really actually could bring freedom to a whole generation of people that have been in bondage for years. Don't despise what you're doing. She was the tent maker. She was the one that stretched out the tent. She was the one that set it all up, and Isaiah 54, when I went here, made me think of her. It made me think of the ezer, or the first line of defense, the woman in the home, praying over her home, asking God to bless it, making sure that if the enemy comes in, he doesn't come to live, he comes in to die.

Isaiah 54:1–4 (KJV) says,

Sing, O barren, thou that didst not bear; break forth into singing, and cry aloud, thou that didst not travail with child: for more are the children of the desolate than the children of the married wife, saith the LORD. Enlarge the place of thy tent, and let them stretch forth the curtains of thine habitations: spare not, lengthen thy cords, and strengthen thy stakes; For thou shalt break forth on the right hand and on the left; and thy seed shall inherit the Gentiles, and make the desolate cities to be inhabited. Fear not; for thou shalt not be ashamed: neither be thou confounded; for thou shalt not be put to shame: for thou shalt forget the shame of thy youth, and shalt not remember the reproach of thy widowhood any more.

Woman IS a contender. I know that this was written to the body of the Israelites. This was written from God as the husband to Israel, His bride. So it's written to men and women, but in this context, since it was written to both, and since it was written to Israel, I want to speak to you as the women of God. As the bride of Christ, who may have felt like everything you were doing was not producing anything. That you're barren and you're empty. You see other things flourishing. You see other people and it's like they're taking off and you're just sitting here. I believe that God is calling for the stretch.

Break forth into singing! Break forth into praise! Break forth into glorifying the Lord your God! Cry aloud! Lift up your voice! Stop being so silent! Open your mouth and God will fill it. So many times we sit on the sidelines because we think, *They don't care what I have to say,* but they do. They're waiting for you to open your mouth and cry aloud, "Spare not thou that didst not prevail with child for more of the children of the desolate than the children of the married wives says the Lord."

To the women that feel like they have no place, no name, no vision, and no authority or had no place that God called you to— He said when you finally begin to break forth, the children of the desolate will be more than the children of the married woman. You will have more abundant fruit born in the earth than those who you have seen baring it for all these years. That is a powerful thing.

Scripture says, "Enlarge the place of your tent, and let them stretch forth the curtains of your habitations. Spare not. Lengthen thy cord, strengthen thy stakes." I truly believe the Lord is saying, "Stretching is coming." He is inviting us into a new place with Him, from the glory of the old place to the glory of the place He is taking us to, because we learned that as a woman, we're not just born of man to be his companion, and to be his helpmeet, but we are a direct reflection of the Lord God Almighty in the earth. That our life is the proof that He is. God is talking to us women and telling us that we are a direct reflection of Who we behold and we are transformed in the same image that we see, which is His image, the image of Christ, the image of the glory of God. The more we see Him, the more we are transformed into that image from glory to glory to glory. We are always changing, and we are always evolving. Not a modern-day evolution, but a spiritual evolution. We start out as babies, then toddlers, then kids, then we start going through that weird phase between a kid and a teenager, then we're a grown up, and then we're like a grandma in the spirit. But we are constantly evolving, and the more we grow, the more we look like our Father. So the Lord is inviting us into a place where He is wanting to stretch us more.

He's wanting us to stretch out our place of habitation. What is our habitation? It's the place that we live. Where are we living? Are we living in our comfort zone? Are we dwelling in our safe space? He is telling us to stretch out and make room. Make room for what you're doing. Make room for growth. You know when we have kids and our kids grow, we have to buy them new beds, because a small bed isn't going to fit a teenage boy anymore. You have to get him a bed that is appropriate for his size. And you change beds from the crib, to the toddler bed, to the kid bed, to the big bed before they ever get there so that they are not ever cramped up in a space. We change plants from one pot to a bigger pot, not when their roots get so matted up that they can't possibly take it anymore. You want to keep the roots from getting bound up, so you replant it and repot it before it's time. And then when the plant reaches capacity, you get an even bigger pot and you re-plant it again. Why? Because you want it to grow, and you want it to thrive. That's what God is saying right now! He wants us to re-pot ourselves. It's the same soil, it's the same Word, it's the same fertilizer; it's just a bigger area. He wants us to allow ourselves to be something bigger than we are right now. Not because He wants us to be bigger, but because He wants to be bigger IN us.

There is a fine line between being the woman of God fully that He created you to be, and letting the enemy come in and twist things to make it about you, to make it about pride. So when I said He wants us to grow, He does, but it's not about us. It's about Him in us and how big in us He can be. We're making room not for ourselves, but we're making room for ourselves to be bigger in Christ and Christ to be bigger in us.

"I'll break forth on the right hand, and on the left, and I shall inherit the Gentiles and make the desolate cities to be inhabit-ed. Fear not for you shall not be ashamed, neither shall you be confounded, for you shall not be put to shame." I want to go here because it's very important in the growing aspect. I've been seeing a lot of people who start coming out of their shells, they start to navigate the gifts of the spirit and hear the sound of God's voice, but the common denominator in all of those people is them being afraid that they're going to mess up, do it wrong, embarrass themselves, or embarrass God. He says it twice here, "Fear not, for you shall not be ashamed." Obey God and stop worrying about what it's going to look like. When you start stepping into what God has for you, are you going to mess up? Absolutely. Will you know it immediately? Yes, you will. Will you learn from that? Absolutely. Experience teaches us more than books or people ever could. Why? Well, I know that fire is hot because they told me that it's hot. I know that the stove is hot because my mom told me not to put my hand on the stove when it's red. But until I burnt myself for the first time, I didn't know. Experience lets us know not to do that. People telling us leaves that doubt in our minds. Are they making that up? Is that really how it is? But if you experience it, then you know.

It's like the woman at the well. When Jesus came, He told her all the things that she had ever done. In the Bible, it says that she ran into the city and she said, "Come, see a Man who told me all things that I have done" (John 4:29). They came out and they began to give their lives to the Lord. But in verse 39, the people that she brought to Jesus began to turn around and said they came because of what she said, but now they believe because they've seen it with their own eyes and they heard it with their own ears. She helped them get to this place, but they didn't believe because of *her* anymore; they believed because they now knew for themselves.

And so, for you to ever get to the place of hearing and understanding that God has a bigger plan for your life, He's trying to stretch you, He's trying to grow you—until you allow yourself to stretch and experience that, you'll never know it to be true. So you can sit on the bench of your life and you can feel that tugging from God, and feel the rattling and shifting inside of you, but you're never going to know it unless you let yourself go there. And you can't go there until you wipe out that fear. You're going to get it wrong, but you don't need to have fear of getting it wrong. Instead, you need to have a reverent fear of the Lord that keeps you in check.

I have people ask me all the time if I'm scared to get in front of people and talk or preach. And I always answer that I'm nervous. Of course, I get nervous. It's not a light thing that the Lord has asked me to do, so I have to be careful to make sure I don't say the things that I want to say, and make sure that I am saying the stuff that He wants me to say. And I hope that the nerves and the reverent fear of God never goes away. But if it is fear to the point where I am crippled and I can't even open my mouth, that is not from God and has to leave in Jesus' name. I'll probably read a word wrong, and I'll probably pronounce it wrong. I'll probably stumble because my brain and my spirit is working faster than my mouth can keep up. But most of the time, people don't really care. It's about people giving you grace, so that way, when it's their turn, even when they stumble on their words, you can give them grace. Y'all can laugh for a second, laugh with the joy of the Lord, then get back to the point and back to the good stuff, and the deep things, and the revelation, and everything will be fine. And you will not be ashamed. God is not going to make a mockery of you. He's not raising you up to make you be the town idiot. He's raising you up to speak as the oracles of God. He's raising you up to pray and to speak out the things that you see, and to invoke change, and to bring life to the people around you, to take the body that you're in and take it to the next level.

There are so many visions that are in my heart and in my head for the people that God has surrounded me with and put underneath my care, but I can't go there until they wake up to the fact that God can use them. One Sunday morning, I saw people finally coming alive to their purpose. We were singing and worshipping, and people just started coming out of the audience to the altar and giving their lives to Christ and bringing their burdens. I saw people on the platform singing, dropping their mics to go down and pray. I saw people from the congregation come up front and pray and wrap people up and love on them and lead them in the prayer of salvation and asking people if they knew Jesus. And it never made me less of a leader because I wasn't praying for everybody that day. It just made the body of the church function like it's supposed to, and nobody looked like an imbecile. Nobody was ashamed, and people were getting saved. People's burdens were being lifted, and God was getting the glory. All because people were waking to the fact that He is stretching us, and He's asking more of us, and we can, because "I can do all things through Christ who gives me strength." If He called us, He's going with us. We're not alone in this thing, so it's fine. And I just wanted to tell you that everything's fine. God using you is not going to upset the whole flow of the earth. It's fine. In fact, it's more than fine. It's going to be phenomenal when all the people of God begin to wake up and realize that it's going to take everybody. The harvest is bigger than what one person can bring in. So that stirring that you feel is because God is saying, "The children are about to come. The harvest is coming and your arms are about to be so full, and everybody's arms are about to be so full, so get up." It's okay to have more than one singer in the congregation, more than one intercessor, and more than one preacher.

"Neither will you be confounded." *Confounded* is utter confusion, and the enemy wants to keep us in that confusion and make us question whether it's God talking to us or not. If the enemy can keep us in a confounded state, we will never move forward. But God is telling us that if we will just take one step, He will remove all of that. All of the warfare that's going on inside of our minds, He's telling us that if we will just keep stepping toward Him, He will obliterate all of that for us.

"For you shall forget the shame of your youth, and you shall not remember the reproach of your widowhood anymore." After tackling fear, I think the very next thing that stops us is the shame of who we used to be. We think because of who we used to be that we're not worthy or we're not capable of being what God would have us to be, and that's just not the case. It's not about who you were, it's about what He's done in you. It's okay. You're going to be alright. Who you were doesn't matter because what He's done is greater. Forget what used to be, because you're not that woman anymore. You might have some of those memories, but you have those memories so you can minister to someone else. You have just enough so you can tell someone that you know how they feel, because you were once there. But not enough of the shame of your youth to continue to be there when you've been bought with a price, saved by His grace, washed in His blood, and sanctified by the Holy Spirit. You're not that girl anymore, you're not those mistakes, you're not those choices, you're not any of those things. You are blood-bought. You are redeemed. You are the daughter of the Most High God. You walk in His authority and in His power that He has given to you to use for the purpose of His kingdom. We have faith that when we're fighting, we're fighting a winning battle.

The enemy's trying to tell us that we're losing all the time, that we're not taking any ground, we're not making any progress, we're the same old same old we've always been—and he's a liar. God didn't put us in a fight that we couldn't win. Every battle that He's ever put you in is because He knew you could overcome it. Maybe not with your own strength, but with His. He'll let us have it and have at it. Do you know, there are times that God will turn people over to a reprobate mind, but I don't believe that that's the situation for anybody that I'm writing to right now. We keep bashing our head against the wall because we won't receive it. Not because we don't love God and we don't want to conform to His ways. We just don't receive. We haven't let it sink in yet. That's not rebellion. That's just, "I don't know how to do this yet, so God's going to be patient with me until I can get it figured out." So know that there are two different approaches to receiving what God has for us: there's rebellion ("I'm just not going to do it period") and then there's ignorance ("I'm not sure how to do this, so I'm just going to keep going the way I know how to go until I get it").

Let's take a look at 1 Corinthians 3:1–9 (KJV). It says,

And I, brethren, could not speak unto you as unto spiritual, but as unto carnal, even as unto babes in Christ. I have fed you with milk, and not with meat: for hitherto ye were not able to bear it, neither yet now are ye able. For ye are yet carnal: for whereas there is among you envying, and strife, and divisions, are ye not carnal, and walk as men? For while one saith, I am of Paul; and another, I am of Apollos; are ye not carnal? Who then is Paul, and who is Apollos, but ministers by whom ye believed, even as the Lord gave to every man? I have planted, Apollos watered; but God gave the increase. So then neither is he that planteth any thing, neither he that watereth; but God that giveth the increase. Now, he that planteth and he that watereth are one: and

every man shall receive his own reward according to his own la-
bour. For we are labourers together with God: ye are God's hus-
bandry, ye are God's building.

Here we see that Paul is saying that when we are so focused on ministers, what they're doing, how they're doing it, blah, blah, blah, that is carnality. We are living in a performance-based world. We're not living in the kingdom, because if we were living in the kingdom, we would realize that it's not about pastor so-and-so, it's not about Pastor Cody, it's not about all the people in all the churches and all the things. It's just about you doing your part. If you're doing your part and I'm doing my part, God's getting the glory and He's bringing forth the increase. He said Paul is nothing. Apollos is nothing. They're men. If you're people-focused, you're not kingdom-minded. You're carnal; you're not spiritual. No matter how much you want to profess that you're spiritual, if you're focused on people, you're not spiritual. You're focused on the carnal realm. It's not about how much I do; it's not about how much you do. It's not about if I'm doing more than you or less than you or whatever. We are fellow laborers with God. We are working together with God. We are His husbandry. We are His building. We're all together in this thing.

I'm not responsible for Paul's part, and I'm not responsible for Apollos' part. I'm responsible for my part. Sometimes when we look at people, we say, "Well, their part is way bigger and my part's insignificant." No, you're just in a different phase of your life than someone else who's been doing it longer or wanting it longer than you have. If you look at it as if God has given you an assignment specific to what only you can do, you'll have a shift in perspective. If He says to you, "I want you to pray for these three people," and that's all He's told you to do, that's enough. Pray. Be faithful to pray for those three people. Don't look at someone else and start thinking, "Well, this one pastors a church, she does a Bible study, she ministers in two jails, and all I do is pray for three people." You automatically feel less than because you're comparing yourself when there's no need to do that to yourself. God did not call us to be each other. He called us to be like Him. I'm not striving to be you and you should not strive to be me. Strive to be who Christ has called you to be. Strive to be more like Christ today than you were yesterday, not more like someone else. I don't need to strive to be some famous pastor or worship leader. I can look at their ministries and I can glorify God for what He's done in their lives. But that's not my goal.

You know, when we look at people, we should admire what God is doing in them and the fruit that He's bringing forth. We should glorify God. But being like other people is not the goal. Christ is the goal, to look less like me and more like Him, to act less like me and more like Him, to obey the words that proceed forth out of His mouth. Yes, I do follow other people. We have pastors, we have leaders. We follow them as they follow Christ. When you stop following Christ, I'm not following you anymore. If I stop preaching the Word of God, stop showing up. If I stop following Christ, and I start getting way out there, and I start doing some craziness that's contrary to the Word of God, even if you love me, pray for me and RUN! Save yourself and your family and run. You have full permission, no explanation needed, alright, but please do pray for me and don't leave me in a crazy place without interceding for my soul.

First Corinthians 3:10 (KJV) starts,

According to the grace of God which is given unto me, as a wise masterbuilder . . .

It's worthy to pause here in order to grasp that God has given you a certain amount of grace. Grace is not like faith. We know that every man is given the measure of faith. We all have the measure. Everybody got the same amount. You didn't get a little bit of faith, and I got a bunch of faith. We all got the same measure. It's one measure, as the Scripture said. If we are all given the measure of faith, then it's what we do with that faith that determines how big it grows or how safe it stays. "We all have the same grace" is different because our assignments are different. So you're going to need more grace to do all these things than I will for the little thing that I'm assigned to at this moment. God is going to put grace on you as you need it. As you grow, He trusts you with more things when you're faithful with a few things. That's when God makes you ruler over many things.

He will give you the grace that you need to do whatever He places in front of you to do. If you get into a ministry you don't belong in and you don't have the grace for it, it will chew you up and it will spit you out. When you don't belong somewhere, you won't have the grace to fulfill what needs to be done. People look at me and they say, "I don't know how you do what you do." It's the grace of God. That's all. I don't know any other explanation for it. It's just His grace—according to the grace that God gave to me. It's personal. God has given you the amount that you need for what He's asking you to do as a wise master builder.

I have got to be smart. I have got to be wise. Not wise in the ways of this world and not smart as in "I know how to do the pythagorean theorem, and I know how to do trigonometry, calculus, and physics." I have to have common sense about what's going on, and I also have to have ears to hear the Spirit so I'll know what God is saying. I have to be able to look and diagnose the situation. Is this safe for me to go here? Probably not. Should I do this? No, I should not. What is God saying to me and how do I put all those things together?

First Corinthians 3:10 (KJV) continues with this:

I have laid the foundation, and another buildeth thereon. But let every man take heed how he buildeth thereupon.

Let every man take heed how he builds. That means, be watchful. Be guarded, not in the sense that you keep everybody out, but that you set healthy boundaries for yourself and for other people, so you don't over extend yourself when you don't need to be and have yourself all shot out where you don't know which way to go, or if you're coming or if you're going. The people that say, "You know what, I love you, but I'm going to get back to you whenever I can"? Or they shoot a text that says, "I got something going on right now, but I promise I'll get back to you," or "My schedule is full, my plate is full. As soon as I can get an opening, I will put you right in here"? I know those people. And guess what? All of those responses are okay. Why? Because you're using the grace that God has given you wisely. You're not using it up. You're not depleting it, but you're staying within the bounds of what He's given you to be able to accomplish the work that's in front of you.

First Corinthians 3:11–15 (KJV) says,

For other foundation can no man lay than that is laid, which is Jesus Christ. Now if any man build upon this foundation gold, silver, precious stones, wood, hay, stubble; Every man's work shall be made manifest: for the day shall declare it, because it shall be revealed by fire; and the fire shall try every man's work of what sort it is. If any man's work abide which he hath built thereupon, he shall receive a reward. If any man's work shall be burned, he shall suffer loss: but he himself shall be saved; yet so as by fire.

While I was pondering and meditating on what the Lord was trying to tell me, I could see a big concrete foundation. We know that that's Jesus Christ. There can never be another foundation. God might tear the whole house down, but the foundation will be saved, because everything we do must be built upon Christ.

In the real world, concrete has to have a time to cure before you can build on it, right? You can't just pour the foundation, then go standing up stud walls. Why? They'll fall over. They'll sink down into the concrete. It won't be right. Everything will be unlevel and be weird. So when you get saved, you're not just going to launch out in the ministry, because your salvation has got to sit for a little while with you. You got to get cured, so to speak. Not cured, as in from sickness; cured as in solid. Your focus needs to be "Jesus loves me. He chose me because He wanted to, not because of how I will perform or how much I will produce." Get the basics right, so that you're not struggling later on in your Christian walk.

Are you new in your walk with Christ? If so, it's okay to just be settled on understanding your salvation, what that means, and what that looks like. What did Jesus really do for me? Let that cure. When you get solid, and you know who you are in Christ, then you can start building. You're not going to fall behind. Receive permission to be where you are and get what you need before rushing yourself to move to what's next.

After I saw the foundation, in my spirit I saw that once the foundation had cured, walls started going up. Then, I had started drying it in and was about to add a second story. I thought to myself, *This is the right way. I've done exactly what the plans called for. It looks like a house, a habitation. It will hold me and other people also. This is good.* Yet, there are times where if we're not careful, we try to start with the second story before we have ever built the first level. We must go in the progression that is going to make for a sturdy, solid house. Christ is always going to be solid, so must what we build. If it's not, we will have to build it over and over again until it's right. Why spend the extra time and money doing it over and over again, when we could just be patient and do it right the first time? I've got to build according to the plan and with the right materials if it's going to work like it's supposed to.

When I went to another country on a mission trip, I saw a lot of houses built from sticks, straw, and palm fronds. Shelter was needed, and those are the only materials that these people could access, so it was all just thrown together. When the wind blows, that mess blows down. Not because they didn't want it to work, but because what they used wasn't capable of withstanding the elements. Spiritually, if you're going to build, build out of gold and silver and precious stones. Gold has to be melted down. There's a whole process. You have to melt it down and pull all the impurities off of it. Then, you have to put it in a bowl and wait for that hot liquid to harden up. You have to let it set for a little bit, and then you can solder other things on top of it.

Applying this to our lives requires us to examine everything. It's not that we have the wrong ideas. We just try to get ahead of ourselves, because we think, *I have to get this done. If I don't get this done, God's not going to love me.* He gave you a word, but He might want you to sit on it for a while and let that word get solid in you. The Lord told me to launch a certain ministry in our church, but it didn't start the day He told me to launch it. There was preparation that had to be done. It was six months in the planning stages before we ever broke ground. Collaborating with those who were going to help, hearing ideas from everyone and really dissecting them to see which ones we wanted to act on and which ones we needed to toss. Everything had to be right. Once it was right, God gave the permission to launch. We could start because now there were people in place and enough people to help work it, and one person wouldn't be overwhelmed trying to do it all.

You know, He told me when I was a child, when I was eight years old, that I was going to pastor a church. I was 32 years old when that word became evident to the outside world. I held that word inside my spirit for 24 years before I never saw the evidence of it in my actual life. Just because He speaks doesn't mean that you have to go right out and do it. The reason we're not okay with waiting is because we still have those roots that are performance based. We feel like if we don't immediately take action when He speaks to us that somehow He gets the impression that we don't love Him or we're ignoring Him. Not so, sis! If you heard it, you just have to let it sit, and then when it's time, He the Lord will make it happen. He says that all the time in Scripture: "You don't understand what I'm doing right now, but at the end, you'll see that there was a purpose and there was a reason."

Ecclesiastes 3:1–10 (KJV) states:

To every thing there is a season, and a time to every purpose under the heaven: A time to be born, a time to die; a time to plant, and a time to pluck up that which is planted; A time to kill, and a time to heal; a time to break down, and a time to build up; A time to weep, and a time to laugh; a time to mourn, and a time to dance; A time to cast away stones, and a time to gather stones together; a time to embrace, and a time to refrain from embracing; A time to get, and a time to lose; a time to keep, and a time to cast away; A time to rend, and a time to sew; a time to keep silence, and a time to speak; A time to love, and a time to hate; a time of war, and a time of peace. What profit hath he that worketh in that wherein he laboreth? I have seen the travail, which God hath given to the sons of men to be exercised in it.

In verses 1–2, God showed me an incredible truth that I want to share with you. Most of us are always looking for times and seasons, but God is looking at things and purposes to everything. There is a season and a time to every thing and every purpose. So "purposes" have times and "things" have seasons. It's not always time to be born. If you're constantly being born every single day, you're probably not in season. What I'm saying is if you're planting, and you never come out of planting, you're never picking. You're never plucking up what was planted. If you're always killing, there's never a healing. If you're always tearing stuff down, there's never a building up. If you're always crying all the time, you can't get out of that weeping season. God doesn't mean for you just to weep for the rest of your life. If you're always laughing, your stomach is eventually going to ache. He wants everything in balance. We can take anything to the extreme and God doesn't want that. He wants it and us well-rounded.

If there's no other foundation that any man can lay than that which is Jesus Christ, then let's look at His life. His life had cycles too. He wasn't always in warfare. If you're always in warfare, something's off. Christ was in the wilderness when the enemy came and stood in His face. Then you don't see Him at war again until He gets to the garden three and a half years after that. Sweat becomes blood. That's warfare. Not the random everyday little nuances of life. Yes, little random things happened along the way, but He spoke to whatever it was. He spoke and demons left. There wasn't a fight. He was walking in authority, and He was empowered. He was healing the sick, raising the dead, healing the blind, raising up the lame. There's a season of warfare, and then there's a season of rest. There's a season that you rest and you just do the ministry. You do what God's graced you to do, and then the closer you get to the cross, there'll be warfare again.

We're all going to go through these cycles until Jesus comes, or until we go where He is. He's going to let us go so far, and then He'll refine us. After refining us, He will add gifts and blessings to us. The further you go, there's going to be more fire and more refining. In that process, He puts His finger on the problem areas. You would have never been able to see it, because all the other stuff (the dross) that burned was in the way. But now that it's gone, you're going to see the issue. It'll be something new, something you haven't dealt with before. So don't get twisted, don't get tripped up, and don't feel like you're a failure. You're just a work in process. There's a Scripture that says for him that has a ministry, let him wait on his ministry.

Let him wait on his ministry. Just because God called you to do something doesn't mean He's going to send you out tomorrow to do it. You just continue studying to show yourself approved as a workman unto God, rightly dividing the word of truth. There are so many people right now that are out professing Christ and have put themselves in arenas and ministry that they don't belong in because they still can't rightly divide the Word of God. They're killing people with the Word that's supposed to make them alive. That performance-based mentality that can't accept the fact that He just loves us because He does. I didn't earn it. I didn't deserve it. He picked me. There's nothing I can do about it. I can't change it. I can't pitch a big enough fit to make it go away. I can't do enough or be lazy enough to make His love more or less. What is true for me, is true for you.

We are contenders because of His grace, love, and favor. We are builders, planters, preachers, intercessors, and warriors! We have been trained in our experiences whether mundane or extraordinary. God is using all of that training to culminate for His purpose and/or thing He chose us to fulfill. We are not the underdogs we have been made to believe that we are. We have a fighting chance! We are fighting from victory and not defeat. So shake off the dust, apply the lessons learned, and walk forward—out of the wilderness—with power and authority and be the champion you have been destined to be!

CHAPTER SEVEN

The Capable Woman

W HO ARE YOU? You are capable. You are capable of affecting change. And I'm excited about this one. I'm excited about all of them, but this one in particular. The definition of *capable*, according to Webster, is that you have the ability, the fitness, or the qualities necessary to do or achieve a specified thing. You're able to achieve efficiently, whatever one has to do, and you are competent.

In this chapter, I really feel that God wants to speak to us and let us know that whatever task He has put in front of us, we're capable. We can achieve it. We have everything we need to get done what He has placed in front of us. We're going to begin in Romans 8:28–32 (KJV). It says,

> *And we know that all things work together for good to them that love God, to them who are the called according to his purpose.*

For whom he did foreknow, he also did predestinate to be con-
formed to the image of his Son, that he might be the firstborn
among many brethren. Moreover whom he did predestinate,
them he also called: and whom he called, them he also justified:
and whom he justified, them he also glorified. What shall we
then say to these things? If God be for us, who can be against
us? He that spared not his own Son, but delivered him up for us
all, how shall he not with him also freely give us all things?

This passage of Scripture is very familiar. I'm sure a lot of us
have heard at some point, especially if you've grown up in church
or been in church any length of time, that "all things work together for good to them that love God and them who are called
according to His purpose." When He says all things, that's what
He means. Not just good things, but the horrible things, the sad
things, the painful things, the hurtful things, the things that bring
you joy, the things that bring peace, and the things that bring turmoil and chaos and war inside of yourself. All of that stuff, every
bit of it. If you love the Lord, He will take your experiences and He
will work them together, and He will bring good out of anything,
because that's who He is.

"To them who love God and them who are called according to
His purpose." In the very beginning of this book, we talked about
how we needed to go back to our beginning, because if we were
ever going to correctly identify ourselves and correctly be able to
see our future, we had to change the lenses by which we saw our

beginnings. And I feel like these passages, this little passage of Scripture here, really touches on the message of Chapter I that we did about going back to the beginning and seeing how He knit us together in our mother's womb. We weren't accidents, we weren't unwanted—maybe by people we were, but not by Him. He designed us so that we would be here for the purpose that He had for our lives to accomplish. We also learned that we are a reflection of Him. If you see me, you should see Him. We all have different shapes and faces and things, but the glory of God is the same in all of us.

"For whom he did, foreknow"—which means that it goes back to my beginning. He knew me before I ever was formed in my mother's womb— "He also did predestinate to be conformed to the image of His Son." When it says that He predestined me, a lot of people think that's a scary word. There are people who believe that He just predestined some people for heaven and predestined some people for hell. If you believe that, I'm not knocking you, I'm just going to tell you that I don't believe that, because the will of God is, according to Scripture, that all men would be saved and that all would come to the full knowledge of the truth. But we have this funny little thing that He's given us called free will. We get to freely say yes or freely say no. There's nobody that the Lord wants to go to hell. There's no one on this planet that God created in their mother's womb, just saying, "Yep, that one's going straight to hell, and this one's going to go to heaven." That's not what I believe. To be predestined means to be predetermined or foreordained. Basically just saying that you were predestined, that He ordained you to do a thing and He wants it to happen, but it's up to you to come into agreement with His desire for your life. You can agree or you can disagree, but it doesn't change the fact that He wants more for you. He wants more of Himself for you. He wants more of His will for your life.

"Whom he did foreknow them, He also predestined to be conformed to the image of His Son." So He foreordained that we would become a reflection of the image of Christ on the earth. That it would no longer be me, but it would be Christ that lives in me, and that He might be the firstborn among many brethren. He didn't just say you, or He didn't just call you, or foreordain you, or predestined you to become the image of Christ in the earth, but He wanted you to have that relationship with Jesus so that you could be the firstborn among many. That by your salvation, by you walking and living out your faith and doing what He's asked you to do, it brings others to Himself. It works in a multiplied way, and not just in one thing.

"Moreover, whom he did predestine, them he also called, and whom he called, them he also justified, and whom he justified, them he also glorified." A lot of people say they feel the call of God, or they've been called by God, and all of those things are true. We all have been called. In the New Testament, Jesus said many are called, but few are chosen. I've always said the difference between the called and the chosen is that everyone gets called, but the chosen are the ones who say yes to that call. And a call is nothing more than a divine invitation. An invitation to salvation first, and then an invitation to an office, or gifting, or whatever you would operate in through the power of the Holy Spirit.

So, number one, we are invited to salvation, and once again, we do have the ability to say, "Yes, I would like to be a part of that" or "No, I don't." And then after salvation, He says, "I have a little something more that I would like for you to do." Maybe it's to speak His word? Maybe it's to stand in the gap, pray, and intercede? He's got this task ahead of you that He would like accomplished. And sometimes it's not that He's just calling us to a position; sometimes He's calling us into a task. He's calling you not just to a position, but He's calling you to a work. There's a work that He wants to accomplish. There's a mission. He's calling you to a mission, not necessarily like a missionary, but He's calling you to His mission that He wants to accomplish in the earth at a certain point at a certain time, and He's inviting you and saying, "Hey, I would really like for you to be a part of this. I'm really drawing you on the inside." And some people will say, "How do I know that I'm called?" If you feel the sense of urgency to a certain thing, or you feel drawn, or every time you're trying to think about something else, your mind just goes right back to this one thing, it's usually evidence that a call is there. Whenever you're drawn to something like that, I would pray into it and would ask Lord, "Why does this keep popping up?" There's a good chance that He wants you to participate in some part of it.

"And them he did predestinate, them he also called, and whom he called, them he also justified." *Justified* means that He has made me righteous. If He gave you an invitation, and you accepted the invitation, He then justifies you by the blood of the Lamb. He justifies you by wrapping and clothing you in the righteousness of God, which is in Christ Jesus. Once you have accepted salvation, it makes you qualified to work for Jesus, to speak for Him, to do whatever in His name. You now walk in an authority that you didn't use to possess, but now you do, because Christ has given you power and authority, not just forgiveness. When you receive salvation, it's a big package, it's a whole bundle. It's not just this one thing. It's a whole bunch of huge things wrapped up in the package called salvation.

"Them he justified, them he also glorified." Which means that He places honor upon you, or He esteems you highly. When He looks at you, He doesn't just think, "Well, that's just her." The world might do that, and they might just say, "Oh, well, she's no big deal." But when He looks at you, once He's called you, once He's justified you, He looks at you and He's like, "She's perfect. She is perfect for what I've called her to do. She's exactly who I wanted. There's nobody in this world I could think of that would do a better job than she would." So many times, I think we let what people say, or how people treat us, take away from the fact that God honors us, that He looks upon us with favor and with great joy and and He glorifies us in the sense of not just that we're honored, not just that we are esteemed, but the glory of Christ, the light of His gospel, the light of who He is, is then transformed into us, and we possess that light. It's not our own, it's His, but we get to carry it, and that light is all around us all the time, no matter how many people want to cover up their eyes and pretend like it's not there. The Lord always sees it, and He always knows it.

"What shall we then say to these things, if God be for us, who can be against us?" And I feel like that is one of the main things that stop us from knowing that we are capable—the thoughts, opinions, and the actions of other people. It's not always the things that they say. It's their body language, it's the way you know when you're being brushed off. And it causes us, if we're not careful, to doubt the ability that God has given us, to doubt the vision that He has given us, to doubt our capabilities. But people don't get to decide that. They didn't call you, they didn't justify you, they didn't redeem you, they didn't glorify you. None of those things were given to us by people. They were all given to us by God, and if they were given by God, people can't take them away. The only way they get taken from us is if we forfeit it in our sadness, or in our pain, or in our hurt. We can lay it down and walk away from it, but the gifts and the callings of God, they're without repentance. It doesn't mean that it's without repentance on my part. It means that when God gives you something, He gave it to you, and He's not sorry about it, and He's not taking it back. So if you lay it on the ground and you walk away from it, He's not picking it up and saying, "Well, I didn't want that to happen anyway." No, He's going to leave it right there, and Christ is going to intercede for you at the right hand of the Father, and He's going to be like, "Okay, we need to do something. You need to get her back at herself, so she'll come back around. We need to corral her in so she'll come back and pick this up, because we're not taking it back. We gave it to her on purpose, for purpose."

"If God be for us, who can be against us, he that spared not his own Son, but delivered him up for us all. How shall we not with him also freely give us all things?" I wasn't going to add this verse at first, but the more I got into this, I thought, *You know, if He did not leave Jesus without, why would He leave me without?* It makes absolutely no sense. Sometimes we feel like He's going to leave us without forever. But if He gave His Son, it would be foolish—and God is not foolish—to not finish the work that you began in your children. It would be foolish to not provide for the needs of the legacy of Jesus Christ and the earth and the active work of the kingdom. Why? Why give up your son and then just quit? He's not going to do that. And so I think we need to keep that in mind.

In Isaiah 54:17 (KJV), it says,

No weapon that is formed against thee shall prosper.

I know we hear this all the time, but it's not about just hearing the Word. He said He needs us to be not just a hearer of the Word only, but He needs us to be a doer of the Word. And you say, "Well, how can I do this word?" You can receive it, and you can let it be an active part of your thought process, that when the enemy comes, instead of being like, "Here we go again" and receiving all the fiery darts, that at some point, we would lift up our shield of faith and we would say, "Okay, enough is enough already. And you know what? You're not going to hit me anymore. You can just hit this shield, because I'm done." No weapon formed against you shall prosper, and every tongue that shall rise against you in judgment, you shall condemn. You get to call down the tongues of the people who speak against you and say things against your life. You know God placed you where He placed you on purpose, for His purpose. You're not living out your own agenda.

There are times in my own life where I'm afraid sometimes to speak up for myself because of the fact that the position that the Lord has placed me in is so taboo in the region where I live that I feel like sometimes I just have to tread lightly, because I just need to be happy to be here. But the Lord said that part of my heritage as a daughter of God is that if there is a tongue that rises up against me in judgment, I can condemn that thing! I can speak out when it proceeds forth out of their mouth. I get to say, "You know what? That's not correct, and I don't receive that in the name of Jesus. And you should be ashamed for saying that." That's not outside of the realm of what we're allowed to do as Christians, but also as women of God, who are called by God, who have been ordained by God and set apart for His holy work. Not just because there's not a man to fill the position, but because from the very beginning, as we have already discussed several studies back, that God intended from the beginning that man and woman should walk together and work together in the kingdom of God. Everybody gets to do a part and that's just the way that it is. We all get to do a part. I'm not called because a man failed to step up. I'm not where I am because a man had better things to do. I'm where I am today because before I was ever formed, He wanted me right where I am, right at this moment!

Colossians 2:6 (KJV) says,

As ye have therefore received Christ Jesus the Lord, so walk ye in him.

"So walk ye in him." Stop walking in the power of self and walk in the power of Christ. We become defeated, we become pressed down and broken, a lot more easily when we walk in the strength of ourself. But as we have received Christ Jesus the Lord, we need to walk in Him. Rooted and built up in Him, not rooted and built up in our strength and in our ability. Rooted and built up in Jesus and who He is, and what His Word has said, and what it's spoken, not only about Him—because His Word testifies of Him because He is the Word—but also what He has said about us as individuals, about this whole entire study.

We're rooted and built up in Him. We're established in the faith. We're not wishy washy. We're not one way today and one way tomorrow. He desires us to be steady in our faith. There's a lot of turmoil in the earth. There's a lot of up and down coming out of our leadership. But the Lord is saying He needs us to be steady. He doesn't need us to roll with the roller coaster of this world, and let our faith be up today, down tomorrow. He just needs us to stay solid.

One time, we were preaching at Holmes county jail, and a man was closing us out. He said something I've been saying for a while now, about being balanced, about the whole counsel of the Word of God, which kind of birthed this study in general about who we are. Not just who they say we're allowed to be, but what does the whole counsel of the Word of God say about women? This man was talking to the guys at the jail, and he said, "If you have too much Spirit and not enough Word, you'll blow up. If you have too much Word and no Spirit, you will dry up. But if you have the right amount of Spirit balanced with the right amount of Word, then you'll grow up." I thought that was so powerful. I've never heard it that way before, but it really resonated with me that we have to have the proper balance of walking in the Spirit and walking in the Word, and a knowing of the Spirit and a knowing of the Word, as well. And the two of them, coupled together, keep us on this walk that we have in Christ.

Colossians 2:7–8 (KJV) says,

Rooted and built up in him, and stablished in the faith, as ye have been taught, abounding therein with thanksgiving. Beware lest any man spoil you through philosophy and vain deceit, after the tradition of men, after the rudiments of the world, and not after Christ.

I feel like this is also what God has been reinforcing. The fact that when we did Titus 2 woman and Proverbs 31 woman, that He was busting through the myths. He was busting through the traditions and the rudiments and the vain philosophies of people and how they have interpreted and skewed things to fit their agenda and their narrative and how they want things to operate instead of what God wants. It's as if He's saying to us, "It doesn't matter how many times they say these things, you know the truth, so you just dwell in the truth and let the chips fall where they may. But don't ever step out of walking in who I am and who I've called you to be to fit yourself back into a mold that I delivered you from, the mold I freed you from." It's important that we remain in Christ and not in the philosophies and traditions of men. Vain philosophies are lies. Hopefully people aren't saying lies on purpose, but they're just repeating lies that they've been told throughout generations. But sometimes people are just flat out lying because they want to manipulate and they want to control. But either way, He said, "I'm the way. I am the truth. I'm the life. You shall know the truth. The truth shall make you free, and whom the Son sets free, is free indeed." So why be entangled again with a bunch of lies that don't need to govern our lives?

Colossians 2:9–10 (KJV) says,

For in him dwelleth all the fulness of the Godhead bodily. And ye are complete in him, which is the head of all principality and power.

You're complete in Him. You are whole. You are very capable. You are very much equipped. You have everything that you could possibly need because you have Christ Jesus, and by the Spirit of God, He is living on the inside of you!

Colossians 2:11–12 says,

In whom also ye are circumcised with the circumcision made without hands, in putting off the body of the sins of the flesh by the circumcision of Christ: Buried with him in baptism, where-in also ye are risen with him through the faith of the operation of God, who hath raised him from the dead.

So you've been buried with Him, and your old life is buried in Christ, and you have been brought up in resurrection life. The resurrection power. The same power that resurrected Jesus from the dead is the same power that is operating in you. And if it's enough power to bring a dead man back to life, it's enough power to do whatever the task that God has set in front of you! You can't shortchange yourself anymore and think that it's just beyond you. Because, yes, in a sense, it is beyond you. It's beyond your flesh. It's beyond your person. But it is not beyond the power that is on the inside of you. Greater is He that is in you. And the enemy comes and he beats us down and pushes us, and we stand for as long as we can, and then he pushes us some more until we are finally just like, "Good grief." But you are still capable. The power didn't go away. You just sat down for a minute. So catch your breath and stand up and do what God has asked you to do, because you are capable.

We're going to talk about Esther, Ruth, and Mary the mother of Jesus in this chapter. We've talked about the warriors. We've talked about those who come in and they fight and they contend and all of the things. But now we're going to go into more of the soft-spoken warriors. But they are warriors nonetheless. What most people probably would want us as women to be are these three main ladies. They like to exalt them a little bit higher because they're less invasive, and their approach is slightly less out there, but it matters just as much. That quiet strength that we as women possess sometimes is just as powerful as if we had our swords blazing and just letting it all hang out.

Esther 4:14 is probably one of the most famous passages for women of God. You see it on T-shirts, necklaces, notebooks, and pens. This Scripture is everywhere. But just a little background information: the Jews were hated, especially hated by a man named Haman. And this is just the short synopsis of it all. Haman is a guy that serves the king at this point in time, and I believe that he was demonically driven. I believe that Satan had ahold on that man, because when you can hate a people so badly that you want nothing more than to take their lives, that's demonic. I mean, there are people that hurt my feelings, you know, and I might want to hurt their feelings back, but I don't want to kill them. I don't want to take the breath out of their body. If it comes to steal, kill, and destroy, then it's satanic. That's demonic. That is an agenda that is straight out of the pits of hell.

Haman was trying to kill all the Jews in Esther's time and season. The closest thing that we would be able to relate to that, I believe, would be Hitler and the Holocaust, except Hitler actually got far, when Haman got stopped in his tracks. I believe Hitler got so far because there was not an Esther to rise up in that generation. I believe that God had laid it on somebody's heart to step in and save, but they became afraid. And then the Lord raised up a country who would say yes and come in and defend. It never should have gotten to the point that it did, but because the times and the seasons were worse, and because people get so calloused and comfortable, they just accepted it. One of the sayings in this country that I hate the most right now is, "It is what it is" and "It'll be what it'll be." And I know that people say that to kind of take some of the anxiety and the worry off of them, but it also breeds a mentality that "it's whatever," and it's certainly not just whatever. If God's laid something on your heart, it's not whatever. "It is what it is" is an excuse to not have to act. And I wish we would do away with that altogether, but that's just a personal thing.

So Haman is trying to annihilate the Jews. If he annihilates the Jews, then there is no lineage for Christ to come. And as we look at all of these women today, I want you to see that every woman that we will talk about in this study, her mission has everything to do with getting Christ into the earth, which is also the mission that we have as women today. No, we're not going to physically bare the Messiah in our bodies and birth a baby. Somebody already did that. That part's already done. But everything about the mission that God has called you to is to get Christ in the earth, into the people that are around you, into the governments, into everyday life, into your workplace, into your children, into your grandchildren, into your spouse, or into whoever you come in contact with. Your mission is about getting Christ into the earth. So if Haman has his way, and he annihilates the Jews, where does Christ then come?

The king had a wife. Her name was Vashti, and she refuses to come and perform for him. She just says, "I'm sick of this. I'm not doing it." He bids her to come. She doesn't come. She gets excommunicated, and sometimes, if you don't want to play the role that everybody wants you to play, you're going to get excommunicated, but that's okay. God had a plan for her life, as well. She gets taken care of. It doesn't matter that people reject you. God still has a plan for you, but in her rejection, it made way for God to be able to get Esther to the throne. There was this great, big process for bridal selection, and Esther got chosen. Her name was Hadassah. That was her Jewish name, but they changed her name to Esther, to kind of put her into hiding, because they snuck her in. And she has to go through all these processes, purification processes and all the things. And she has been chosen as the wife of the king.

Then they discover Haman's plot to kill the Jews. And throughout all the things that they're asking her to do—to go before the king and plead for the Jews—she's just like, "I cannot. I cannot do this. This is beyond me. This is a whole nation and not just one person." But her uncle Mordecai was like, "You have to do this."

Esther 4:13–14 (KJV) says,

Then Mordecai commanded to answer Esther, Think not with thyself that thou shalt escape in the king's house, more than all the Jews. For if thou altogether holdest thy peace at this time, then shall there enlargement and deliverance arise to the Jews from another place; but thou and thy father's house shall be destroyed: and who knoweth whether thou art come to the kingdom for such a time as this?

It's like a direct reflection of Romans 8. He foreknew you, and He predestined you to be a mighty strong deliverer for His people. Because it's God's will that this nation and this people thrive because He's got a plan, and there's an end game to this. And if you're not going to do it, He's going to leave the call laying on the ground, but you will be the cause of your own death. You'll be the cause of your own death if you don't say yes to Jesus or yes to the call of God on your life at this point in time. If you don't say yes to God, then your house is going to be destroyed, you and your house, and there's going to be bloodshed. But eventually the Lord's going to raise up another deliverer. So you can either do what God has asked you to do, or you can bench yourself and you can watch someone else do what you're supposed to be doing, and you can die on the sidelines.

I know that that's really intense, but that's a thing, and I feel like God is telling us as a people that you can be discouraged if you want to, or you can figure out a way to believe and to trust Him, and He'll see us through this thing, and we can accomplish what He's asked us to accomplish—or we can sit back and we can pout, and we can watch somebody else, because what He wants to accomplish is going to come to pass one way or the other. He'd rather have you, but if He has to go elsewhere, He will.

And Moredecai said, "What if you were brought into the kingdom for such a time as this?" And I want to say it's not even a "what if" question at this point anymore in our own personal lives. It's this: You were brought here. You were knit together in your mother's womb on purpose, for purpose. You are here at the right time, at the right place, in the right season, to enact change. You are capable of making a change in the earth, wherever the circumstance is that He's placed you in. You are capable of doing that. You can because He is, and He's in you, and you can speak the things that you need to speak, and you can put your hands to whatever He's asked you to put your hands to, and you can get on board with whatever He's saying, and it will happen. I'm not going to say it can happen. I'll say it will happen, because that's the kind of faith that we need. It's not, "Oh, well, God might do it." No, He *will*. It will happen, just like He said it would happen. And in Esther's life, she surrendered to that call, and she went.

There were times that she had to just bust in the door—and you couldn't just walk before the king whenever you felt like it, because he could kill you if he didn't extend out his scepter to you. But there came a time that she just had to bust in there and do it, and she didn't think that she had the strength, and she didn't think that she had the capability, and she didn't think that the favor of God really did rest upon her life, until the time that she had to test it and see it really does. And she knew, "You really did call me. You really did set me here because anybody else, they would have just gone away. But I'm here, and I'm alive, because You went before me and You made a way when I didn't see a way. And when I was afraid, I stepped anyway. You were right there."

A battle ensues with Haman and Mordecai. And Haman makes these gallows for Mordecai because he wants to kill him, because he knows that Mordecai has got a plan that's going to ruin his plan. So it was one of those "I've got to get you before you get me" kind of things. But because of Esther's faithfulness and her obedience to God's plan, she goes before the king. She invites him to all these dinners. She has several dinners, and at the end of these dinners, she tells the king what she wants, and what she wants is her people. She called everyone to a great fast. Everybody fasted, everybody prayed, and God moved. God moved on their behalf because of her obedience. And Haman was actually killed on the gallows that he had intended for Mordecai. And when we fulfill the call of God, and when we walk in the capabilities that He has given us, and we exercise those things, the enemy will be destroyed in the trap that he set for us. He will be the one that's embarrassed and put to shame. God's people will never be put to shame when they put their trust in Him. It may feel like it's going to be shameful, but it's not. He will come on the scene with a mighty hand and an outstretched arm, with fury poured out. That's how He will rule over His people. He will contend with those that contend with you. He will mess with them that are messing with you. Don't worry. He's got it, so it will all work out.

I thought it was really cool that at the end of Esther, we see the king write letters and he says all the Jews are going to be saved. He says, "We're not going to kill these Jews. We're going to leave them alive." So he sends out all these letters, and Mordecai is writing letters, and then at the very end, we see in Esther 9:29 (KJV), it says,

> *Then Esther the queen, the daughter of Abihail, and Mordecai the Jew, wrote with all authority, to confirm this second letter of Purim.*

So not only did she get to walk in the favor of God and walk in the capabilities He gave her. He also let her write letters. It wasn't just kings and important people writing them. He elevated her to a status where she got to write, and she got to decree a thing, and I've never paid attention to that, but it spoke to me. When He places us in the seat of authority, He seats us there. We don't just get to do some of the things, we can do all the things, and I just thought that was super powerful and worthy of mention and recognition.

We're going to back a few books and dive into the story of Ruth. Ruth is a Moabite. She is not Jewish by descent. She marries one of Naomi's sons. Naomi, her husband, and her two sons flee Bethlehem because there's a famine in the land, and they end up going to the Moabites and living with them. When they go to the Moabites, Naomi's husband dies and both of her sons die. All she has left in the world are her two daughters-in-law, Orpah and Ruth. She tells the girls to go back to their people, that they just need to go back, get away from her, and go live their own lives and not worry about her. She will figure it out. So Orpah gladly kisses her mother-in-law, saying, "There's nothing left for me here. I'm going back." But it says this in Ruth 1:14–18 (KJV):

> *And they lifted up their voice, and wept again: and Orpah kissed her mother in law; but Ruth clave unto her. And she said, Behold, thy sister in law is gone back unto her people, and unto her gods: return thou after thy sister in law. And Ruth said, Intreat me not to leave thee, or to return from following after thee: for whither thou goest, I will go; and where thou lodgest, I will lodge: thy people shall be my people, and thy God my God: Where thou diest, will I die, and there will I be buried: the LORD do so to me, and more also, if ought but death part thee and me. When she saw that she was steadfastly minded to go with her, then she left speaking unto her.*

After this, they traveled back to Bethlehem. And I want to say this: never underestimate the power of showing Christ to someone who is lost. Being a light to those around her probably wasn't a part of Naomi's agenda. They were fleeing from a famine. Naomi and her family weren't out on the mission field, but something about the way that they lived their lives, and something about the way that they made God important, really affected this heathen girl. So much so that she said, "There's something about you. Your God will be my God. Your people will be my people. I don't want to live the way that I've been living, and I want more of this. You may not have a husband to give me, you may not have any possessions to give me, but your God is enough." And because they shared Him with her, and they imparted that belief system into her life, she is one of the great-great-great-grandmothers of Jesus Christ.

This heathen woman saw God, and He used her to raise up the inheritance back to Naomi's family, and she didn't think that she could do this stuff. All she thought was that she was just so happy to be a part of this faith and just so happy to be a part of this belief system. But she thought, *What really can I do? It doesn't really seem that important that I'm going into Boaz's field and I'm just picking up leftovers.* But her obedience and her willingness to just do whatever was asked of her brought her from picking up leftovers in a field to picking up handfuls that were left behind on purpose, which led to her owning the field that she gleaned in. And God raised her up to not just be a widowed heathen that was brought into the faith by this mother-in-law, but to being the wife of Boaz, to birth out Obed, who birthed out Jesse, who birthed out David, and out of David's seed came Christ of the throne of David, and of His kingdom, there shall be no end. That's pretty incredible.

Ruth 4:13–17 says,

So Boaz took Ruth, and she was his wife: and when he went in unto her, the LORD gave her conception, and she bare a son. And the women said unto Naomi, Blessed be the LORD which has not left thee this day without a kinsman, that his name be famous in Israel. And he shall be unto thee a restorer of thy life, and a nourisher of thine old age: for thy daughter in law, which loveth thee, which is better to thee than seven sons, hath born him. And Naomi took the child, and laid it in her bosom, and became nurse unto it. And the women her neighbours gave it a name, saying, There is a son born to Naomi; and they called his name Obed: he is the father of Jesse, the father of David.

So there are some times in our lives when the Lord calls us that it's not just about saving a people or saving ourselves. Sometimes it's about redeeming an inheritance that had been forfeited or lost. There is kingdom authority that has been established in the earth. When the Lord sends an anointing in the earth, the people may leave but the anointing stays behind. For example, when Elijah and Elisha were together, and Elijah got caught up in the whirlwind, God took Elijah, but He left the anointing. The mantle represented the anointing over his life. People leave. God calls people home and they leave. But that anointing remains in the earth. Naomi's sons died, but their inheritance, the thing that they had been promised, it remained behind, and somebody had to redeem it. Somebody had to pick it up and carry it forth. Why? Because that's who Jesus had to come from.

Maybe God has called you to pick up something that someone else has left behind and to fulfill that calling, to pick up the baton and carry it to the next place, to make sure that the race gets finished, make sure that the process gets done. Before Roe versus Wade was so close to being overturned, I was thinking about the process. It could've stopped before the finish line, but because there have been people that have kept the ball rolling, passing the proverbial baton from one age group to the next, it finally happened. You might be thinking, *Well, that's not a preacher thing. That's not a mission. Those people weren't missionaries or preachers.* But like I said, God doesn't just call you to a position. Sometimes He calls you to a work. Sometimes He calls you to an actual mission. And what more would be the heart of the Father than preserving life, than preserving generations?

Some people started on the journey to overturn Roe versus Wade, and they died before they saw the fulfillment of the mission. But just because they died doesn't mean that the vision died. Somebody had to come and finish. There have been women that God has raised up, not just to go to the seats of the nation, to the capitals, and to the courts, but there was a generation of silent warriors all over the world that God placed a burden in their heart to intercede for the overturning of Roe versus Wade. Some women, that's all that they did. That's all that God had placed in their heart. Their mission was to pray it through and birth it out, and they did just that! They may never have physically touched a document or physically signed anything, but they fought a war in the heavens and made sure that the breach was filled in, and that the gap was restored.

Maybe God has called you to a mission similar to this. Never underestimate God calling you to stand in the gap for someone else. You don't know what you standing in the gap is going to mean, not only for your future but for the future of those that you're praying for, and the future of the people that are going to be affected by what you're praying about. It's not just momentary things. He works generationally. He works beyond. His plan is not just a right now plan. It's a huge picture that we can't even comprehend or focus on. We couldn't understand it all, even if we tried. God used Ruth in that kind of a way to affect generations. And because Ruth was risen up in the time that she was, Esther was able to do what she had to do. Because Ruth came, Esther could come. It all works together. When one woman does what she is supposed to, it makes way for the next woman to fulfill her mission because she will be alive to do it! When we live to fulfill our call, we leave a path to purpose behind that others can pioneer. It's a beautiful thing. The kingdom of God is amazing.

Last, but certainly not least, Mary the mother of Jesus proves that women are capable. Luke 1:26–34 (KJV) says,

And in the sixth month the angel Gabriel was sent from God unto a city of Galilee, named Nazareth, To a virgin espoused to a man whose name was Joseph, of the house of David; and the virgin's name was Mary. And the angel came in unto her, and said, Hail, thou that art highly favoured, the Lord is with thee: blessed art thou among women. And when she saw him, she was troubled at his saying, and cast in her mind what manner of salutation this should be. And the angel said unto her, Fear not, Mary: for thou hast found favour with God. And, behold, thou shalt conceive in thy womb, and bring forth a son, and shalt call his name JESUS. He shall be great, and shall be called the Son of the Highest: and the Lord God shall give unto him the throne of his father David: And he shall reign over the house of Jacob for ever; and of his kingdom there shall be no end. Then said Mary unto the angel, How shall this be, seeing I know not a man?

"How am I possibly capable of doing what You have asked me to do?" You know she's thinking it! Luke 1:35 says,

And the angel answered and said unto her, The Holy Ghost shall come upon thee, and the power of the Highest shall overshadow thee: therefore also that holy thing which shall be born of thee shall be called the Son of God.

"How am I capable?" Because the Holy Ghost is going to come upon you, and it shall overtake you, and this baby shall be born of you.

Luke 1:36–45 says,

And, behold, thy cousin Elisabeth, she hath also conceived a son in her old age: and this is the sixth month with her, who was called barren. For with God nothing shall be impossible. And Mary said, Behold the handmaid of the Lord; be it unto me according to thy word. And the angel departed from her. And Mary arose in those days, and went into the hill country with haste, into a city of Juda; And entered into the house of Zacharias, and saluted Elisabeth. And it came to pass, that, when Elisabeth heard the salutation of Mary, the babe leaped in her womb; and Elisabeth was filled with the Holy Ghost: And she spake out with a loud voice, and said, Blessed art thou among women, and blessed is the fruit of thy womb. And whence is this to me, that the mother of my Lord should come to me? For, lo, as soon as the voice of thy salutation sounded in mine ears, the babe leaped in my womb for joy. And blessed is she that believed: for there shall be a performance of those things which were told her from the Lord.

When God calls you to do a thing, He establishes it out of the mouth of two or three witnesses. The Bible says, let everything be established. And the angel of the Lord came and he spoke. And then the Bible says that when Mary went to Elisabeth's house, that when she greeted Elisabeth, Elisabeth was filled with the Holy Ghost, and the Holy Ghost that spoke through the angel of the Lord verbatim, said the exact same thing through Elisabeth to Mary again, without Elisabeth's knowledge. The Holy Ghost spoke through her, and she said, "You are carrying my Lord. You are carrying the Messiah." It was the same thing the angel of the Lord said. "You will birth the Son, His name will be Jesus, He will sit on the throne of his father, David, and of His kingdom there shall be no end." And if there was ever a doubt that she could do this, that word from the Lord, through the mouth of Elisabeth, should have told her, this thing will be.

Blessed is she who believed the Lord, because there will be a performance of the things that He spoke. He watches over His Word. The Scripture says He watches over His Word to perform it. Whatever He's placed on the inside of you, He will see it all the way through. He that began a good work in you is well able to finish it. I'm capable, because I get that from my Father. He's capable and He will. And because He's capable and He will, I'm capable, and I will do all that He has asked of me to do.

They went into Bethlehem after this encounter for the census, and there's no room in the city for them. In the end, she has Jesus in a stable in the back of an inn. She lays Him in a feed trough/manger. I want us to see something about Mary that is like the Lord. He never starts something He won't finish. They don't praise Him as author and finisher, beginning and the end for nothing, friend. We don't just find Mary at the birth of Jesus but also at the foot of the cross. You find Mary seeing Him through life from the beginning, from the day of conception and the day of birth, and you see her in John 19:25– 27 (KJV):

Now there stood by the cross of Jesus his mother, and his mother's sister, Mary the wife of Cleophas, and Mary Magdalene. When Jesus therefore saw his mother, and the disciple standing by, whom he loved, he said unto his mother, Woman, behold thy son! Then saith he to the disciple, Behold thy mother! And from that hour that disciple took her unto his own home.

So she didn't just take the call of God and what He had placed in her lap as "I'm just going to birth this thing." She saw it all the way through. And when we take care of the mission that God has given to us all the way to the end, He makes sure that we are taken care of. Take care of His business, and He will take care of you. We see that when Jesus is no longer going to be walking on this planet in the flesh, and she's at the foot of the cross watching her grown baby die a death for people who don't want Him and have rejected Him, and that she's no longer going to have Him anymore, one of the last wishes that He says before He dies is, "Mother, behold your son, and son, behold your mother." And from that day forward, that disciple took her into his home and took care of her and saw her throughout the rest of her living days. Your end is taken care of from the very beginning! When we're faithful to

God and we step in and fulfill the capability that He has placed on our life, then He's capable to finish the rest. We do what we're called to do in its fullness. In the joy of giving birth, in sorrow, in the pain of death, and in the triumphant resurrection. She saw it in every form, in every stage, and she saw it through to completion. And then God in turn blessed her and took care of her for the rest of the days of her life, and the Lord promised those same things to us.

You are capable because your Father is capable. See the work through to completion. While she was giving birth, He was already at the foot of the cross making her reservation to live out her days in comfort at the disciple's home. He's already made provision for you. He will never not take care of you—especially when you are being about His business! It is my greatest hope that you will be able to put the words of this book into your spirit and go forth and do ALL that God has put within you to do. Don't be afraid. Don't settle. Refuse to live another day letting the plan of God pass you by. Get off the bench. Call for a reset! Go, sister, go! Be faithful in all things. Leave a legacy, and impart every drop of knowledge and wisdom you gain into the women who are running with you, and especially to the women who are coming up behind you.

Woman, who are you? Where once you had questions, I pray you have answers. I charge you to make sure the ones around you and coming behind you don't get caught up in the questions.

Help them make their footing sure. Don't stay silent one more day. Someone is counting on you to fulfill your purpose, so they will be able to fulfill theirs.

Study Questions

Chapter One: A New Beginning

1. The author emphasizes returning to the "beginning" to heal identity wounds. What practical steps can you take to revisit and reframe your own origin story through God's truth?
2. Consider the metaphor of God knitting us together. How does this shape your view of your body, soul, and personality traits—even the ones you've struggled with?
3. The chapter critiques the belief that people can only be good if others affirm them. How have you sought validation from people instead of God, and how can that change?

Chapter Two: The Titus 2 Woman

1. Paul's letter to Titus was written to bring order to chaos. How does understanding that context change how you read instructions for women in Titus 2?
2. How does the story of the woman with the issue of blood illuminate the difference between healing and wholeness? How have you experienced one but not the other?
3. The author critiques performance-based Christianity. How has striving for spiritual perfection affected your relationships with God and others?

Chapter Three: The Proverbs 31 Woman

1. This chapter reclaims Proverbs 31 from being a legalistic checklist. Which traits of the Proverbs 31 woman do you already possess that you've overlooked or dismissed?

2. The comparison between rubies and pearls is powerful. In what ways has your value been misunderstood by yourself or others, and how can you begin to correct that?

3. Consider the roles of provider, intercessor, entrepreneur, and nurturer seen in Proverbs 31. How do these manifest differently in today's context for women?

Chapter Four: A Divine Reflection

1. 2 Corinthians 3:18 says we are "being transformed into the same image from glory to glory." What does "glory to glory" look like in your personal growth journey?

2. The author says we no longer shine with our own light—we shine with His. In what ways have you been tempted to dull your shine for the comfort of others?

3. Consider the mirror metaphor. What does your reflection say today about what you believe regarding God—and about yourself?

Chapter Five: The Ezer

1. The Hebrew word "ezer" is used to describe both woman and God's help. How does this redefine what it means to be a "helper" in your relationships and ministry?

2. Jael used the tools of her daily life (a tent peg and hammer) to destroy the enemy. What are the ordinary tools or skills in your hands right now that God might use for spiritual breakthrough?

3. Reflecting on Deborah, Phoebe, Junia, and others, how does the inclusion of women in frontline leadership roles challenge traditional narratives you've heard?

CHAPTER SIX: THE CONTENDER

1. Paul commends women who "contended" beside him in the gospel. What battles are you fighting today—for your family, your church, your city—and how are you contending?
2. The chapter emphasizes unity between women and with leaders. What unresolved tensions or offenses may be hindering your ability to contend effectively with others?
3. "Help" in Philippians 4 is defined as "assist, apprehend, seize, become pregnant." Which of those postures best describes where you are in your journey right now?

CHAPTER SEVEN: THE CAPABLE WOMAN

1. The author connects Mary's beginning (pregnancy with Christ) to her ending (at the foot of the cross). What mission has God given you that you need to see through to completion?
2. Romans 8:30 outlines a process: foreknown, predestined, called, justified, glorified. Which of these stages feels most real to you today—and which one do you struggle to believe?
3. This chapter contrasts self-reliance with Christ-reliance. How can you practically shift from striving to operating in the resurrection power already within you?

Index

CODY BOYETT is a wife, mother, pastor, songwriter, author and a lover of Jesus above all else. Being His daughter is her most beloved name and position in this life. Her desire is to see lives born again and radically transformed by the power of Abba. She is native to the Florida Panhandle and is waiting with great expectancy for the manifest glory of God to ride in like waves on the shores of the Emerald Coast and to see His glory flow throughout the rest of our nation and the world. "His glory shall cover the earth as the waters fill the seas." Isaiah 60:2

www.ingramcontent.com/pod-product-compliance
Lightning Source LLC
Chambersburg PA
CBHW021827090426
42811CB00032B/2058/J